NAUDÉ

PROPHET TO
SOUTH AFRICA

G. McLeod Bryan

JOHN KNOX PRESS
ATLANTA

Dedicated to
George Okoth Bryan-Doherty
Born in Kenya, April 21; 1977
Whose parents work for the Africa
herein envisioned

Excerpts from the *Pro Veritate* journal and publications of the Christian Institute of Southern Africa are used by permission. Quotations from other writings of C.F.B. Naudé are used by permission of the author.

Library of Congress Cataloging in Publication Data

Bryan, G   McLeod.
  Naude, prophet to South Africa.

  1. Naudé, Beyers. 2. Reformed Church—Clergy—
Biography. 3. Clergy—South Africa—Biography.
I. Title.
BX9595.S63N383   285'.732'0924 [B]   77–15746
ISBN 0–8042–0942–1

CONTENTS

2087826

The Defiant Ones: On the day of their refusal to testify before the Parliamentary Commission, August, 1973. As of October 19, 1977, all five have been served banning orders.

Left to right: The Rev. Brian Brown, Editor Roelf Meyer, the Rev. Theo Kotzé, Mrs. Jane Phakathi, and Dr. Beyers Naudé.

FOREWORD
An American Introduces Naudé to America
by ROBERT MCAFEE BROWN

The Rev. C. F. Beyers Naudé is *a churchman, a pastor and a prophet.* Like most prophets, he is now without much honor in his own church—let alone his own country—because he has tried, as pastor to his people, to be their prophet as well. There is ample biblical precedent for the fact that prophets are not generally well received, and Dr. Naudé is no exception. There may be awards in Chicago, but there are no awards in Capetown.

Once a moderator of the most powerful branch of the Dutch Reformed Church in South Africa, Dr. Naudé came to believe, particularly after the Sharpeville massacre of 1960, that the pro-apartheid stand of his church could no longer be justified. He said so in a memorable sermon that cost him his pulpit, his job, and his place of esteem in Afrikaaner society. It is assumed in South Africa that many leaders of the *English*-speaking churches will oppose apartheid, and they can be "tolerated" because they are numerically too few to comprise a genuine threat. What cannot be—and is not—tolerated is the voicing of such a cry by members of the Afrikaans community, particularly when, like Beyers Naudé, they have been part of the *Broederbond,* a small, exclusive organization with enormous power, standing uncompromisingly for white supremacy in all aspects of South African life.

So, for Dr. Naudé to be a churchman, pastor, and prophet has also made him *a risk-taker on behalf of many.* I have had the privilege of two brief meetings with him. One was in the Capetown airport when I was arriving and he was leaving. He had just come from staff meetings of the Christian Institute (CI), of which he is the head, and a bomb had gone off in the meeting hall shortly after adjournment. Only the inefficiency of the timing device had prevented a tragedy. The second meeting was at breakfast in Johannesburg in the home of a member of Naudé's staff, and the hostess placed her tea cozy over the telephone on the assumption that the special branch of the secret police would be monitoring the conversation, whether the phone was off the hook or not. Bombings and buggings are routine rather than exceptional.

So we can say, in further describing him, that he is *an affirmer of the lordship of Christ and, therefore, a denier of the lordship of Caesar.* In South Africa to say "yes" to the first is also to say "no" to the second, for South Africa is a police state. Political dissent is not tolerated. Every aspect of the society, the church not excepted, is riddled with informers. Those who defy are banned, bombed, or bugged, indicted and hauled into the courts, fined and imprisoned.

Beyers Naudé knows many of these realities from his own past, and he knows, too, that they remain possibilities for the future. It is his positive affirmation of the lordship of Christ that leads to his costly denials of the lordship of Caesar. In his country one has to act without assurance that the undertaking will succeed, with the assurance only that the act must be undertaken whether it succeeds or not. One has to resist even if there is only the likelihood that resistance will not be tolerated.

Another way to put this is that Dr. Naudé, as a *believer in God's love is, therefore, a practitioner of human justice.* How do we embody love in a loveless world? By engaging in the struggle for justice, but by doing so in a manner that continues to be infused by love. Nothing is more taxing today than to attack the wrongness of the viewpoint of an opponent and still retain a sense of his or her humanness.

Can we spell this out more concretely? I believe we can by describing Dr. Naudé *as a provider of space for total sharing and, therefore, a troubler of the status quo.* That seems to me to be a shorthand way of describing the reality of the Christian

Institute of which he is the founder and head. In a land that insists on enforced segregation of the races, the CI has defiantly embodied a space for total sharing. Its staff and membership include Blacks, Coloureds, Asians and whites—to employ the artificial terminology that is legally binding in defining who a South African is. The CI provides a space where these categories lose their meaning, even as a desperate government keeps building ever higher walls of division between classes, races, and churches.

This is a lesson for South Africans, but it is a lesson for those of us who are in less perilous situations as well. And so we can say finally of Dr. Naudé that he is the *exemplar of a courage that challenges others to risk more because he continually risks all.* We must be reminded by Beyers Naudé that South African tensions are a microcosm of world tensions. What is true there in blatant form is true elsewhere in more subtle (and not so subtle) forms.

If in South Africa a tiny white minority has oppressive control over the destinies of a massive nonwhite majority, this is the way it is on the global scene as well. If nonwhite South Africans are not going to accept this unjust state of affairs indefinitely, neither are nonwhite members of the entire global family going to do so. The South African drama is a prelude to an increasingly rapidly unfolding global drama in which the same basic issues emerge. There are not many places from which we can take cues as to what our own proper posture should be, as the global pressures begin to be exerted against *us*—the tiny white minority with so much oppressive power over the vast nonwhite majority. And so, grateful for Beyers Naudé's courage, we can only hope and pray, not only for the vigorous continuation of his witness, but for the possibility that a bit of his courage may rub off on us.

CHAPTER ONE
Cry, The Beloved Country

No country presents two faces to the world more dramatically than South Africa. Visitors, whether a tourist, businessman, space-age scientist, sportsman, or wild life enthusiast, see one face. Their vista is carefully filtered. They fly in, they are entertained, they attend well-staged conferences, they view the scenic sites and lodge and dine at the finest of suburban estates. They get the impression that all is well, that what problems South Africa may have had in the past are being overcome by gradual enlightened improvements, and that the country is as progressive in both technology and human relations as any country in the world. And, if these outsiders travel elsewhere on the continent of Africa, they are likely overwhelmed by how far South Africa is ahead of the other African nations. Moreover, if they come from Europe or America they feel instantly at ease since the predominant social institutions and customs resemble those back home: the multiple-party democracy, the free press, medicine, the theatre, the educational system, the well-attended churches, the judicial system, and the sports. Yes, especially the sports, for South Africa has sometimes been characterized by its three R's: race, religion, and rugby. The visitors come to feel instinctively that South Africa belongs to their part of the world.

Few outsiders have to be persuaded by the skilled propagandists hired by the government to present just such an image. Outsiders who share a radically different perspective are not likely to secure visas, and any outsiders who seek to probe behind the attractive facade into areas beyond the routine tour will find instant barriers erected to thwart their private investigations. Therefore, herded, cloistered, lulled by their gracious hosts, most outsiders are likely to see only one face of South Africa, the face of luxury and liberty.

The other face of South Africa is one of tragedy, suffering and oppression. Millions of its people exist on the edge of poverty, have the most private parts of their lives controlled by petty nuisance laws, and are subject to arrest, detention, and imprisonment for the slightest infractions against the ruling minority. The fifteen million Blacks, Coloureds, Indians, and other ethnic groups are without citizenship rights and live daily in the fear and frustration of a legalized and severely enforced segregation system known nowhere else in the world. While it is true that the indigenous Africans and other imported minorities who are not white have their share of the technological progress and prosperity of South Africa, their proportion is not only strictly contained but is also a mere fraction of the whites. The white person (4 ½ million) has the right of ownership of land in any part of white-declared South Africa (87% of its present territory); he may offer his labor anywhere, enjoy his social privilege at large. No African (11 ½ million) has such rights. The average income per white is approximately nine times more than the income per African.

This policy known as *apartheid* is designed primarily to preserve the privileges of the whites within the nation and has been most effective since the present government came to power in 1948. Since that date, any voices of dissent have been silenced by new government policies consecutively becoming more restrictive. Between 1950 and 1976 fifty-nine laws have been enacted "to protect the security of the State." Variously, these laws dealt with passport refusals, proscribing political parties, detentions, and bannings (both without trial). The last Act of 1976, the Internal Security Act, is the most oppressive. This act virtually empowers the Minister of Justice to imprison a person forever, without recourse to any court of law, provided that in the Minister's opinion such a person is a danger to the security of the state. Thus, white South Africa has given to one man a power greater than that exercised by Parliament or by its highest court of law.

Therefore where one outsider sees the face of the good life of South Africa, another outsider sees the most efficient police state. Big Brother so controls the lives of the majority of the people that they do not even need the rights and privileges of citizenship. They reside in vast ghettos planned and constructed by the state, and Big Brother provides euphemistic names. "Soweto" may sound as if it is rooted in an African language, when in fact it literally stands for South West Township, where over a million Africans are contained and are allowed to "pass" into the white territory only to serve. Whites live in the city, Blacks live in townships. Housing, jobs, education, marriage rights, and the legitimacy of their children, even their beer and the language they speak, are all dictated by the bureaucratic efficiency. "All these provisions are necessary for the Africans to catch up with our civilized ways." "Ethnic differentiation must be preserved because this is where creativity derives." Thus bureaucrats schooled in management and psychological manipulation at the best of universities sit in distant offices and plan the lives of the masses. If totalitarianism is defined as the few who know best deciding the vital necessities for the many who are incapable of deciding for themselves, then South Africa is an advanced totalitarian system.

This system, born of fear and guilt, expresses itself in multiplied rationalizations and constantly revised, more severe attempts at the repression of voices of dissent. After all, the first face of South Africa is that which the ruling minority wishes the world to see. But it is in fact a *minority*. From that *minority* consciousness emerges the ever-present insecurity, its guilt about its present oppressive policies and its fear of the inevitable doom accompanying the future reversal of roles.

There is another face of South Africa, a third face. It is composed of those who have faced up to the illusionary nature of the first face and the harsh reality of the second face. By some inner sensitivity or revelation from a higher source, these persons reject both these images and devote themselves to an entirely new South Africa, one dedicated to true humanity, to justice and to liberty for all. These voices are few indeed, but powerfully loud. Alan Paton, the most world-famous of these persistent voices, though periodically squelched by the powers-that-be and now in his old age rather gloomy about the prospects, writes in 1973 in an essay entitled "On Turning 70":

> In 1938 I was a believer in the resurgence of Afrikanerdom. I could see good in Afrikaner Nationalism. In 1973, I can do so no longer. Its cruelties are insupportable. I could have made better use of my life, but I did try hard to do one thing. That was to persuade White South Africa to share its power, for reasons of justice and survival. My efforts do not appear outwardly to have been successful.

Writing again, this time in September, 1976, following the Soweto riots of June 16, his tone is even more ominous:

> I write not to express my detestation of the policies of apartheid, not because my Government has cruelly and ruthlessly treated its more articular opponents, including many of my friends, but because I fear for the future of Afrikanerdom. I fear it is going to be destroyed and I fear that the process of destruction has actually begun. If so, it began on June 16, 1976, [and I fear] a chain reaction that cannot stop until everything is destroyed.

Paton has spent a lifetime viewing both faces of his beloved country, with deep-felt pathos and compassion, which was first registered in the book that became a world best-seller when first published in 1948, *Cry, the Beloved Country*. Since the publication of that book, there have occurred several uprisings on the part of the oppressed: at the Cato Manor riots of the late 1950s, at Sharpeville in March, 1960, and now the school children of Soweto. In each case the government suppressed them swiftly and cruelly—69 Blacks killed at Sharpeville and over three hundred estimated killed at Soweto.

In addition there have been the new devices of detention and banning. In the detentions alone, from 1974 to 1976, 217 persons have been hustled off to indefinite incommunicado prison confinement, without protection of the courts, without legal advice, without at that stage being charged with any crime, and held for a total of 61.8 years. If measured by the number of family and friends affected by the detentions, the suffering, anxiety, tension, and pain is incalculable. The April 30, 1976, report issued by the Christian Institute estimates that over 20,000 persons have been affected and concludes:

> The effect is beyond calculation at present, but what can be seen is that incommunicado detention of so many people has and will continue to have a considerable effect on the Black Community and will increase their determination to continue the struggle for a more just society in South Africa. (p. 4)

This figure jumped astronomically following the student protests of June, 1976. A Christian Institute report released two months afterward estimated at least 2,600 arrested, many of whom have been held for weeks, having had bail applications refused and then inexplicably released without being charged. On the 10th of August, Mr. Kruger, Minister of Justice, extended the preventive detention sections of the Internal Security Act to the whole of South Africa. Within days some 50 or more recognized leaders of the Black Community were detained. Some of these were held under Section 6 of the Terrorism Act, which allows for solitary confinement and creates the possibility of interrogation under torture.

Paton, in the passages cited above, refers to Afrikanerdom. The leaders who comprise this cultural entity actually consist of a minority of the minority within South Africa, but in the mounting crises of their political reign they have garnered a substantial majority of whites to support them in their policies. Paton refers to them as

> a Christian who is determined to remain a Nationalist, and he has therefore constructed a culture called Christian-Nationalism. It is a culture that judges education, literature, art, morality, religion, law-making, sexual behavior and ultimately thought itself, by the standards of its own tribalism. . . . (They) believe they have been given authority by God, who having created so many separate and different

races, wishes above all things that they should stay separate
and different. And if you have been entrusted with a divine
mission, then surely you must at all costs carry it out.

In other words, Afrikanerdom is a political messianism. And
the good face of South Africa presented to the world is primarily seen as God's gift by his dedicated servants, the Afrikaner
people. Of course, as in the Old Testament, many peoples must
suffer in order that God's Chosen People may emerge. Their
Nationalist-Christian identity demands the absolute loyalty of
the Christian to the God-given goals of the presently instituted
government. Thus the present rulers of South Africa have forgotten they were elected in a democratic process and are claiming their authority as given by God. Their divine mission is
nationhood (what others would call ethnic purity). It is an up-
dated tribalism that pretends the equal legitimacy of all tribes.
But the catch is that they interpret their God-given mission, to
be carried out at all costs, to be the preservation of the supremacy of their own tribe-nation-race irrespective of what happens
in the process to the other tribes.

In the face of that Afrikaner syndrome it is understandable
that, as Paton further observes, there are not many exceptions,
that is, Afrikaners who deviate from this political messianism.
Yet it is not surprising, in the light of the extreme narrowness
implicit in Afrikaner Christian-Nationalism, that directly from
the core of this belief-system should emerge another conception of God's political intentions. The person who has publicly
and decisively abandoned Afrikanerdom and who has moved to
center stage in exposing the two contradictory faces of South
Africa and its government is the subject of this book, Christian
Frederic Beyers Naudé.

At the conclusion of his celebrated trial in November, 1973
—when the Government "against Naudé" won its case, holding
him in contempt for having put his individual conscience above
giving testimony to the Parliamentary Schlebusch Commission
which was investigating his own organization, the Christian
Institute—the Court declared:

After weighing all the facts and circumstances in the case, the Court comes to the conclusion that not one of the excuses offered by the accused can hold good, and that in his circumstances and in spite of everything he acted unreasonably. A citizen of this country, or a citizen of any democratic country, also has a legal responsibility towards the lawful authority of that land. Accordingly he is found guilty as charged.

In the sentencing, the Judge added: "Like all other people you are entitled to criticize the Government's policy—others also do it daily, but there are limits."

What made Naudé's case different from the others was accordingly spelled out by the Court: It occurred within the storm-center of a white-controlled African nation imperiled by its surrounding black liberated nation-states and by the majority of Blacks among its own people; and, secondly, it originated from a citizen of considerable stature and leadership who was altogether a product of the Afrikaner community. Naudé had suddenly emerged as an Afrikaner who challenged Afrikanerdom where it hurts the most.

This fact became more obvious on the release of the Schlebusch Report (167 pages) two years later, in May, 1975, when both the Prime Minister and the Minister of Justice took the occasion to target Naudé as their principal source of irritation. Two days after the release of the report, the Christian Institute was declared an Affected Organization, no longer able to function freely and threatened with extinction. The report itself declared: "(It) will judge the Institute's actions by the generally accepted principle that the supreme authority which has its origin in the juridicial sphere is vested in the State, and will then apply the test whether the Institute's actions and activities may endanger the security of the State." Forthwith, Naudé publicly renounced this "generally accepted principle" and labelled such action "naked totalitarianism, which claims the God-given right over the total life of man, and which the Christian Institute utterly rejects."

Following the riots of June, 1976, he was officially warned, and those around him treated more harshly. Several of his staff were detained: Jane Phakathi, Regional Director in his Johannesburg office, Mashwabada Mayatula, one of his field workers, the Rev. C. Wessells and Vesta Smith, both on his Board of Management. On the 25th of November the security branch of the South African Police raided his offices one more time, and the editor of *Pro Veritate,* Cedric Mayson, was detained.

The government's charge as stated in the Schlebusch Report focused on its main grievance with Naudé and the Christian Institute: "In appearance, in character, and in function, the Institute has become a completely political body with a political destination."

Although the government's charge was literally untrue, Naudé and the Christians he represents could not deny that their interpretation of the Christian gospel and of God's will in history demanded daily political involvement. Typical of Naudé's challenge to the political messianism of the government are these lines from a speech he delivered at the University of Natal, August 25, 1975, just two months after the Schlebusch Report release:

> I wish to emphasize that I am prepared to give my full support to any party or group which comes forward with a call not only to end all forms of racial discrimination but to set aside as totally unacceptable the policy of separate development and to plan the necessary steps for a coming together of the White and authentic Black leadership of the country to discuss and decide the political, educational and economic future of South Africa.

The messianic interpretation of politics held by Naudé and the Christian Institute roots in the biblical prophetic stance that God works within history to rectify evil and to establish the humanity of man, the liberation of all and the healing of the nations. That much of the legal case against Naudé and his supporters is true: they are politically concerned Christians. And that fact infuriates the politicians in power. They cannot brook any criticism or alternative to their own version of political messianism. They charge, falsely of course, that every criticism or act against the government is Communist-inspired, "the work of the devil." That way they prove their own godliness and the godliness of their own political goals.

But what if God laughs in derision at the foolishness of nations? What if he shakes all nations and finds South Africa wanting? That is the insecurity which Naudé's witness implants in the mind of the genuinely sincere Afrikaner Christian Nationalist. And it helps explain more than anything else why their leaders hate him so, and why they hesitate to act against him lest they find themselves acting against God.

One can hardly imagine the pressures to conform exerted by the Afrikaner culture upon one of its members showing signs of rebellion. These pressures were even more compelling in the case of Naudé, for if anybody was the proper child of Afrikanerdom it was he. (This may shed additional light on the government's strangely prolonged toleration of Naudé's rebellion: the most rabid of the Afrikaners cannot believe a true child of the faith will ever turn traitor, and they may entertain the vain hope that he will eventually return to the fold.) From the time of his birth, Naudé had everything in his favor to rise to the top when the wheel of fortune granted the old Boer tradition its opportunity to seize power from the British. The Boers, after their defeat in the Boer War at the beginning of the twentieth century, had been subject to all the humiliation of being forced to swallow the English culture—its language, its economic suzerainty, "the Union" a part of the Empire, and its social institutions. Everything English was good, everything Boer was bad.

Smouldering under decades of English arrogance, the Boer-Afrikaner consciousness not only preserved its integrity but actually expanded. Naudé's life, born on May 10, 1915 in Roodepoort in the Transvaal, the stronghold of the former Boer republics, literally spans the life-cycle of the Afrikaner ascendancy from a suppressed minority to a ruling minority. On one of the few occasions when Naudé has spoken of his first forty-five years, he tells that the bedroom of his birthplace was literally aglow with the fires from the burning houses of his pro-English neighbors, fires set by the Boer defenders.

His father was chaplain to the Boer troops, and served under General Christian Frederic Beyers. From his father's devotion to the general and the Boer cause, the child was given his full name. Significantly Naudé was born in a Dutch Reformed Church pastorium. The dominees assumed the principal role in nurturing and preserving the Afrikaner messianic culture. His father played a unique part in this, insofar as he became widely acclaimed as the first dominee to use the Afrikaans language in the pulpit (instead of Dutch), when Beyers was six years old and then residing with the family in Graaff-Reinet. Naudé reports that he recalls the very preaching of that sermon and the sensation it caused. This was in 1921, and it was not until 1933 that the Afrikaans translation of the Bible finally replaced the Dutch Bible. So Naudé was at the center of the Afrikaans renaissance, where its language was articulated and where its school-teaching dominees guided the shaping of the culture. But of course the English were to forbid the teaching of this coarse, bastard language in the public schools. His father therefore became responsible for organizing the first school in the Afrikaans language in the Cape Province, "die Hoer Volksskool in Graaf-Reinet."

The atmosphere of this school, like all others where the Boer children were constantly impressed with their "differentness," naturally lent itself to an awareness of radically different culture values. With four cultures imposing themselves upon Naudé (he mentions that by the time he was four when his father pastored in Piet-Retief near Swaziland he spoke more Zulu than Afrikaans since he played mostly with African children)—Zulu, Afrikaans, English and biblical—it is not surprising that he now claims these teenage years engendered within his mentality a high degree of criticism, judgment, and alienation. Already his moral sensitivities were being honed, and in the year of his graduation from high school he led five classmates in a school protest.

The following term, 1931, he entered that citadel of Afrikanerdom, Stellenbosch University, taking a B.A. in 1935 and an M.A. in 1937. He admits that during those college years he was not at all sure of what profession he wished to enter. As he looks back now, he identifies two things which cooled his ardor for the church and his father's footsteps: one was the small-mindedness and the corruption that he saw in the church, the other was the low appeal of theology, especially in the light of the DuPlessis affair (a heresy hunt then being conducted by the Dutch Reformed Church against one of its best minds).* Nonetheless, during those campus years he threw himself into several debating clubs, taking in all the "liberal" causes, and found himself actually the organizer of a notorious club which he labelled "Pro Libertate."

Still not certain, he enrolled in the church's Theological School, an adjunct of the University in Stellenbosch, and graduated in 1939. Following his graduation he took an assistant pastorate at Wellington. There he took the fatal step of re-enforcing his Afrikaner convictions and connections—he joined the Broederbond. Looking back, he recalls that his motivation was "so I could serve my people better and also secure positions of influence." The Broederbond, a quasi-secret society functioning underground among the Afrikaners, was dedicated to wresting what power they could from the all-powerful English super-culture. As we shall see, this step was to haunt Naudé the remainder of his life, but at the moment it seemed the perfectly natural thing to do. His father had been one of its founders in 1918.

From 1942–1945 he moved to Pretoria-South, where among his congregation were the Prime Minister, General J. C. Smuts, and his wife. Naudé does not reveal whether this man ever confided in him as a pastor, but it is well known that Smuts'

---

*Of the three White Dutch Reformed Churches in South Africa, much the largest and the one to which Naudé belongs, is called the Nederduits Gereformeerde Kerk, often styled NGK. In 1960 it had over 1,300,000 white members, with affiliate churches containing 550,000 Africans and over 400,000 Coloureds. The Nederduits Hervormde Kerk van Afrika (NHK) had in 1960 about 190,000 white members, and an affiliate with a few thousand Africans. The Gereformeerde Kerk in Suid-Afrika has only about 100,000 whites.

ideas, both on religion and the destiny of South Africa, were unique.

From 1945–55 he was student pastor in the Pretoria University area, and became the first president of the Christian Youth Movement, just organized among the N. G. Kerk of S. A. As such he had the opportunity to travel for 6 ½ months throughout Europe, giving him, as he later admitted, a new perspective on the world.

In 1955 he moved to a church in Potchefstroom, another university town, only this time he was closer to the heart of conservative Calvinism and its endorsement of the Afrikaner Christian Nationalism than ever before. It was here that this half of his life was to reach its zenith, since he was soon elected acting Moderator of the Transvaal Synod in 1958, and Moderator in 1963. He had moved to a church in the suburbs of Johannesburg by then. During those years the entire course of his life was abruptly changed.

What happened? What initiated this radical turnabout? What were the undercurrents already running through his psyche? What were the deciding factors?

Alan Paton, Afrikanerdom's most astute observer, wrote of Naudé's transformation in the following manner, in an article in *Christianity and Crisis,* September 30, 1974:

> I, and many others, would take Beyers Naudé as the proto-type of those white South Africans who when they take Christ as the Lord of Life experience, even if not immediately, an immense emancipation. Naudé was a militant Afrikaner, a Protestant, a dominee, a powerful moderator and, most remarkable of all, a member of that exclusive organization the "Broederbond" which stood for white supremacy and for the overlordship of the Afrikaner in every department of South African life—religious, moral, political, cultural, educational, and even sports. As far as one can see, the liberation is complete. One is forced to conclude—because one does not reach such a conclusion lightly—that this is the work of the Holy Spirit and that Beyers Naudé was struck down on some Damascene road.

Naudé himself has spotted this conversion as happening during these years at Potchefstroom, according to testimony delivered by him at his defense trial:

> For me it was a turning-point in my life, because the night before the final decision was made at the Synod, I had to decide—would I because of pressure, political pressure and other pressures which were being exercised, give in and accept, or would I stand by my convictions which over a period of years had become rooted in me as firm and holy Christian convictions. I decided on the latter course and put it clearly to the Synod that with all the respect which I have for the highest assembly of my Church, in obedience to God and my conscience I could not see my way clear to giving way on a single one of those resolutions, because I was convinced that those resolutions were in accordance with the truth of the Gospel.

The sequence of events to which Naudé here refers pertains to a December, 1960, Consultation held at Cottesloe, a district of Johannesburg, convened by the World Council of Churches and bringing together for the first time the leading Protestant Churches of South Africa into an ecumenical consideration of racism. At that Consultation a number of resolutions were passed, among them one that no one who believes in Jesus Christ should be excluded from any church on the grounds of his color or race, and another that the right to own land where he is domiciled and to participate in the government of the country is part of the dignity of all men. When they became known, the reaction was violent, from the Afrikaans Church circles and the Afrikaans political press in particular. Protest meetings against the resolutions sprang up everywhere, with so much denunciation that when the NGK Synod of Transvaal convened in April, 1961, after long and heated debate, all the resolutions were rejected and the synod even decided to withdraw from the World Council of Churches. At that synod the twelve delegates to the Cottesloe Consultation were given the opportunity to justify their participation and their point of view. The majority of the delegates, faced with the intense hostility of the synod toward the resolutions, gave in. They

expressed either their regret at the fact that it had become clear
to them that they had embarrassed the NGK by accepting these
resolutions, or their willingness to abide by the viewpoint of the
church as interpreted in the discussions at the synod. It was to
this "cop out" that Naudé took exception.

And in so doing, the remainder of his life would be changed.
His public renunciation of his fellow delegates and the collapse
of his church under political and cultural pressures marked him
forever. He had crossed the Rubicon. He was not alone in his
stand; there were other rare individuals who also spoke up, and
who in turn were encouraged by his stand. Moreover, the
repercussions were such throughout the whole Afrikaner community of South Africa that no Christian with a strong commitment among them could rest easy. To return to the transcript
of Naudé's trial:

> I accepted that an event of great historical significance had
> taken place in our Church, which in a certain sense came
> as a great psychological shock to our whole church commu-
> nity and our Afrikaner nation, and it became clear to me
> that it would be many years before the Dutch Reformed
> Church, as an official church institution, would again see its
> way clear to debate and discuss and make decisions con-
> cerning these questions in church meetings in public. This
> brought to my mind a very important question about the
> responsibility of the individual minister and member, who
> was convinced that the opportunity for study, for making
> contact, for discussion among members and ministers of
> the various Churches who saw the need for this more than
> ever before that the question came to mind—what could
> we do to maintain contact on an informal, personal level?

From that moment on, every action, every word that ema-
nated from Naudé would be carefully watched. He had for-
saken his upbringing, he had broken his vows, he had betrayed
his people. His daily life would be exposed; his own person and
family would be hounded, threatened, rejected; his new career
and activities would be misrepresented and undermined; and
he would become the central target of the ruling government.
Sir Robert Birley, the British jurist who edited for the Interna-

tional Commission of Jurists the 1973 trial of Naudé, compared his witness to that of Socrates and Joan of Arc:

> As one looks back through history one notices every now and then some trials when the roles of the participants seem to be reversed: the man in the dock becomes the prosecutor, the prosecutor is in the dock. . . . I feel that the same change is seen in this trial of Dr. Beyers Naudé. It was not done by any kind of histrionics. The tone is quiet, almost gentle. Those who knew him will recognize the man as they read his evidence. Slowly the tables are turned; it is the South African Government and, to Dr. Naudé's obvious deep sorrow, his own Church, who have to answer the charges.

CHAPTER TWO
Why Dost Thou Try Me
Every Moment of My Existence?

In 1960, at forty-five years of age, Naudé was a successful career man within Afrikanerdom, distinguished from the run-of-the-mill Dutch Reformed dominees in their black suit, white tie attire, invariably their uniform, only by his quick rise to office in a patriarchal structure notorious for its undue premium upon age. He had reared a fine family of four children, being married to Ilse, had had several successful pastorates, had been a member of the Broederbond for twenty years, and had been elected acting Moderator of the powerful Transvaal (Johannesburg area) Synod. He had excellent family and in-law connections and was beginning to be known through his country as a promising leader of his subculture. Outside South Africa he was unknown.

Yet when the World Council of Churches convened in Nairobi in 1975 his name was mentioned more than any other person's as the one Christian who exemplified courageous witness to Christianity in the contemporary world. How, then, this radical turnabout? From Sauline zeal as a model of Afrikaner piety and patriotism to Pauline conversion to the lordship of Christ within the total culture? From a conformist, culture-Christian to becoming the key spokesman for Christ against the currents of South Africa and the main target of the persecuting authorities? From a law-abider to a lawbreaker? What happened to cause him to exchange a quiet comfortable suburban white man's existence for a life of imminent danger, one of tumultuous conflict and misunderstanding, one with worldwide repercussions and significance?

In this chapter we shall endeavor to trace the development of his spiritual consciencization, his pilgrimage from a loyal boy of Afrikaner Calvinism to a profound understanding of the Christian's prophetic vocation to his times.

In his later self-appraisals Naudé has fixed upon his Potchefstroom days as the beginning of his renewal. By some strange coincidence I first encountered Naudé twenty years ago during his days in this very university village of Potchefstroom, way off the beaten track of mainline South African cultural traffic. Looking back, I must confess that I instantly noticed something different. He exhibited no evidence of the normal sagging associated with middle-age mentality. Quite to the contrary, he expressed unexpected interest in me, the outside world, and in particular what an outsider thought of Christianity in his country. In this out-of-the-way station I had been shuttled to his house because the few other brains in town seemed put off by my insistent probing and were glad to rid themselves of an outside inquisitor. On the contrary, Naudé became my inquisitor, pressed me for all I was worth, over the couple of days and then offered to drive me to my next appointment in a nearby village, which, incidentally now as I look back, was a black theological school in which Naudé expressed peculiar interest, especially at whether I would spend the night between their sheets.

I realized even that early that Naudé was cut from a different cloth. I had made it my special business to get to know the Dutch Reformed Church leaders, their theologians, and while their recognized professors such as Ben Marais, B. B. Keet, and J. C. Kotze had all written books devoted to the specific question of race and religion, they left me with the impression of a doctrinaire approach. Naudé was alive. I noted in particular the keenness of his interest, his concentration riveted on the other person in the dialogue, his intensity of purpose, his transparency of motivation, and his extraordinary sensitivity. But the scattered misgivings he shared with me on that first occasion scarcely prepared the listener for how far afield he would go.

What began as an uneasy conscience about racism ended in

a challenge to the modern Behemoth, the superstate. What began in a relatively minor decision reached life and death proportions, and in the process the terms of the contest between Naudé and his culture shifted considerably. At first he believed, naïvely, that it was possible to combine being a loyal dominee and an ecumenical, concerned Christian. He envisioned a reasonable public debate gathering more and more people into the pluralistic planning of an alternative future for his country. He had at that time little conception of the direction or the difficulty of the path he was being led down. It seemed to him at the time such a little thing, indeed the only right thing to do; how could he anticipate that it would be instrumental in overturning his world?

As we attempt the unraveling of this man's witness we are amazed at the slow beginnings of his awakening, composed of such little bits of disturbances, a chance meeting here, a teacher's words there, an upsetting encounter. But all these combined created a great bolt of lightning, and he found himself caught in a maelstrom not at all to his liking. God had led him into strange paths. As may be guessed, he found himself many times afraid, afraid for the consequences of his new beliefs, afraid for his very life later on. Among these bits of disturbances were the questions of the students at his university pastorates, the reading of Professor Ben Marais' book, *The Color Crisis of the West* (University of Pretoria), and advising the younger ministers of the church during the years of 1958 and '59 when he was acting Moderator.

Of Marais' book he reports that it was the first time that he was forced to study the scriptural statements on race, and "it became totally clear to me what the Bible asks of the Church and of a Christian on race relations. But I was afraid of the consequences." In counseling the young missionaries of the NGK who were working on the Reef (the extended gold-mining area around Johannesburg), he later discloses the effect of their alarms on himself.

> One in the compounds, one among the Coloured community, and one among the Indian community, who shared their concern with me, because they said that there was an

increasing tension developing between White and Black in
South Africa; and for the first time in my life they brought
to my attention a number of situations of injustice of the
non-White, partly because of our legislation and our policy
of *Apartheid,* causing them serious problems in their ministry, and in their preaching of the Gospel.

Because I could hardly believe this I asked them to
arrange a number of meetings with leaders, Coloured and
African, but also in a number of cases one or two Indian
leaders, where I could meet them to hear from them personally what the position was and on what their objections
were based. This happened and it made me realize that
here in our country we live in a situation where the Whites
on the one hand live their secure, secluded and in many
respects closed lives, where an immensely large section, if
not the largest section of our White population, are not
aware of the feelings, the experiences, the pain and the
tension in the hearts and the lives of our Black communities. At that time, however, I did not take the matter any
further, although I knew that at some time or other an
answer would have to be given.

But, as we have mentioned before, the decisive jolt in
Naudé's mind-set occurred with the gathering of the ecumenical body of the Dutch Reformed Churches throughout the
world at his little town of Potchefstroom in 1957, the Reformed
Ecumenical Synod. He reports: "Although I was not a delegate,
I attended because of my intense interest in the theological
problem which was developing around the Church and race. I
attended a number of open meetings and took serious cogni-
zance of the report and the decisions of the Synod." In testimony given at his 1973 trial, he continues to reveal the impact
of this meeting:

At this Synod in discussions which took place and also in the
personal discussions which I had with delegates, many of
the convictions which had become clearer to me during my
previous years of theological study now crystallized. I
should possibly mention that it was particularly in four
different areas where I sought for light, based on the light
of the Gospel. Firstly, the whole question of the unity and
diversity of the human race; secondly, on the unity and
diversity of the Church on earth; thirdly, the responsibility

of the Church in the different areas of human society; and, fourthly, the necessity for the Church to play the role of reconciler in situations of serious tension. . . . I discovered that the truth of the Bible conveyed to us clearly that God created all the nations of the world in one blood, and that the fact of the different residential areas was not a fixed premise, a pre-destination, an unchangeable pre-destination of God, but a historical development and therefore that the unity of the human race is fundamental for the calling of man on earth.

Significantly these very themes were to reappear continuously throughout Naudé's new public stance following the cataclysmic happenings to his career in 1963. But at this moment his pilgrimage was slow and cautious. "I was afraid to proclaim the full implication of this message, because I realized something of what it would entail for my position and my future." The road which Naudé was to travel was long and hazardous, and not unexpectedly he was reluctant to take it. Many a day and night thereafter he was to fear not only for his family and future but for his very life. Terror became a way of life for him. It is therefore understandable that on some occasions he would over-react. He seems to have been particularly afraid of being banned. When the Schlebusch Commission was "breathing down his back" he reports "that I could draw but one conclusion . . . that I must begin to prepare myself as in other cases to expect a banning order." In the trial his defense counsel led him into the following testimony:

Naturally it came to mind that if it could happen to these young people [the NUSA students who were just recently banned] then the possibility of my being banned also surely had to be faced.

And how would Naudé accept such a harsh decree?

In spite of such a possibility and as a result of my own point of view, I would continue my task fearlessly. I must tell you that in the work which I do I accept that such a step may be taken against me, but that in spite of the possibility that such a thing could happen, I am convinced that I should give my Christian witness in this country fearlessly and with love.

What began with the Ecumenical Synod in Potchefstroom bore much fruit in the later Naudé, in spite of his fears. Ecumenical meetings, meetings which brought together not only the branches of one church or the denominations of Protestantism but also the Roman Catholics and all the variations of the African churches, became Naudé's organizing forte and his principal platform to address the world. His appearances at these conferences, consultations, and conversations followed in rapid-fire succession: Cottesloe, 1961; founding of the Christian Institute, 1963; Lunteren, Uppsala, South African Council of Churches "Message," all in 1968; Geneva and Ulvenhout, 1969; World Council of Churches Central Committee, Addis Ababa, 1971; All-Africa Church Conference, Lusaka, 1974; the World Council of Churches, Nairobi, 1975. All these felt the imprint of Naudé's hand either directly or indirectly. Throwing himself immediately into the sponsorship of the Cottesloe Consultation between the World Council of Churches and the Churches of South Africa in 1960 (Naudé was one of the hosts), he stayed constantly embroiled in these invigorating sessions, right up until his latest call (1976) for a National Convention consisting of representatives from all peoples and dealing with the future shape of South Africa. Finding himself forced from his own pulpit and ordination in time, even forbidden by the synod to serve as an elder in a local congregation, he turned to his new platform, erected from the wreck of the institutional church to which he belonged.

Naudé had never imagined his tragic alienation from the church he loved more than anything else and to which he had devoted the best years of his life. But, ironically, the leaders of this very church conspired to wreck him, and, even worse, the official position of the church ran counter to the universal moral conscience in its endorsement of racism. Thus the most radical step of Naudé's life was forced upon him at the very outset of his twice-born life, a step he would have preferred never to have taken and forced upon him all too suddenly and altogether without proper consultation with him.

He was left spiritually naked, without a church home. This is not to say that he abandoned the church. Quite the contrary, he threw himself upon her mercy more than ever. Only now he viewed the church at three levels: the church militant, primarily in its ecumenical functions, both those already established and that part he was to organize; the local congregation of any denomination which, in spite of its failures, even denials of the full gospel ethic, functioned as a spiritual center; and the great fellowship of God's living saints whom he met all over the world and who in turn sustained him by prayers, by financial and legal materials, and by other concrete means of encouragement. This latter he came to appreciate more and more and to identify as the "confessional church." His official church home may have abandoned Naudé, but in his abandonment he found what he called the real Body of Christ.

The initial event in the alienation happened as follows. By 1959 Naudé had moved to a prosperous suburb of Johannesburg and had organized and was pastoring the Aasvoelkop Church. As we have noted, while acting as Moderator of this particular synod Naudé had begun to engage in ecumenical affairs both within his own denomination and among the wider Christian fellowship. With the collapse of Cottesloe, he and others likeminded were dismayed. "After the decisions of the Synod," to use his words, "the membership of these ecumenical study circles dropped sharply, but a number of the ministers and missionaries continued to meet regularly, sometimes monthly, bimonthly, to discuss these questions. But it was clear that from the official side little could be expected by way of any lead that the church would give, at inter-church level, to maintain this contact and to extend it. Those of us who were convinced that this should be done maintained contact and sought to continue with the discussions in these ecumenical study circles."

From this modest beginning emerged the new instruments of Naudé's ministry. In April, 1962, this small group established an ecumenical monthly journal, named *Pro Veritate,* and

Naudé was named editor. The instant reaction of the Dutch Reformed Church was vehement against such a biblical witness in the sphere of the sensitive area of race relations, which clearly was the focus of the journal's concern. Other denominations scarcely took notice of its formation as they looked upon it as mostly a family fight within the DRC. When it became apparent that the synods meeting within the ensuing year would not recognize its legitimacy, the same loose association of ministers and laymen met on the 15th of August, 1963, to establish the Christian Institute. In September, 1963, Naudé announced his decision to accept the directorship of the Institute, even at the loss of his ministry, to the members of his congregation. It was to be "at the loss of his ministry" because by that date his official church had made it clear that, if he continued in those directions, he would be stripped of his clergy rights. One must remember the significance of the coincidence that at this very time Naudé was Moderator of the synod, and in proceeding he petitioned the synod to retain his status as a clergyman but was refused.

Looking back upon that crucial moment, before he was obliged to preach his valedictory sermon to his congregation, he now says, "This was the most difficult decision which I have had to make in my life." Using as a text Acts 5:29, which reads as follows: "We must obey God rather than men," Naudé declared in this sermon:

> Consequently the choice facing me is not primarily a choice between pastoral work and other Christian work or between the Church and Pro Veritate, or between the Church and the Institute. No, the choice goes much deeper: it is a choice between obedience in faith and subjection to the authority of the Church. And by unconditional obedience to the latter, I would save face but lose my soul.
>
> By joining the Christian Institute, I am not leaving the Church. On the contrary, I wish, through the Institute, to serve my church in the wider ecumenical content, even if my church today does not officially see it in this light, or so desire it. Nor am I abandoning the ministry of the Word—

for this very reason, I applied for permission to retain my status in order to show my church that I did not wish to be anything other than a minister of the Word. Concerning the decision of the Examining Commission I would only say that I regard it as unreasonable and unjustified—a decision which cannot be upheld on the basis of ecclesiastical policy nor founded on precedent. And so I pray that the day may soon dawn when this decision will be rescinded.

The organizational staffs of both were thoroughly representative of the various church bodies of South Africa, but naturally composed of those gravitating around Naudé. They included whites, Blacks and Coloureds, all three Dutch Reformed bodies and seven other Protestant denominations (later embracing Roman Catholics as well). Admittedly the journal issued more directly from the DR churches. Illustrative of this is the fact that its first issues were largely in Afrikaans but running double copy on important articles so as to include English. In its middle years it was about half and half. Its latest issues still contain some Afrikaans copy but this evidences the loss of Afrikaans readers, the very ones to whom it was first aimed. Its first editorial stated: "For some time a number of ministers and members, mainly of the three Dutch Reformed Churches, have felt the need of a Christian monthly paper which would aim at approaching and discussing vital problems of the Church and the community in the light of Scripture." Its headline article was exposing *apartheid.* On the board of seven members was only one English-speaking clergyman. But it rapidly attracted attention beyond the scope of the initial editorial and gathered readership and contributions from widely divergent sources, becoming one of the most genuinely grass-roots ecumenical journals published anywhere in the world and containing information obligatory for any person seeking to be informed on South Africa. Its modest beginnings and its limited subscription list to the present day belie its tremendous impact upon South African thought.

The Christian Institute from the start had a wider base, and throughout the years has considerably extended its representation from all parts of South African Christianity, especially welcoming Blacks on its staff and its Board of Management. Naudé has summarized its work as follows:

> The Christian Institute is an organization of individual Christians from all Churches in South Africa, with four main aims and objectives. In the first place, to give a more visible expression to the biblical truth of the unity of all Christians, all believers. In the second place, to relate the truth of the Gospel more immediately to the questions of our daily existence and to make its meaning more clear to its members and to all who wish to know it. In the third place, to act as a group of Christians who wish to help bring about reconciliation between the widely divergent, divided and conflicting groups of Christians of different Churches and colours in our country. And in the fourth place, to offer the services of our members to any Church or group of Churches who wish to make use of them to give a better expression to the Kingdom of God in South Africa. [From transcript of 1973 trial.]

Certainly the governing party and the ruling church of South Africa never underestimated the innovation. And the government began its attack at once, with a campaign of smears, innuendos, planted rumors, and direct criticism in the party papers. Within two months after the organizational meetings of the CI, Naudé in the name of the Executive Committee was forced to issue a public statement:

> The C.I. considers it necessary to issue a statement in the light of the unfounded attacks which have been made against it from various quarters and the malicious rumours which have been spread.... [There follows a paragraph by paragraph clarification of the CI's relationship to communism, to multiracialism, to political action, and to its sources of income. It concludes in no uncertain words:] There is an obvious pattern of similarity in the methods that have been used by the various bodies which have attacked the Institute and in the content of the arguments and imputations which have been employed to substantiate these allegations. One is therefore faced with the irresistible conclusion that a centrally-directed campaign must have been organised somewhat behind the scenes.

The influence of the Christian Institute is feared, wholly unnecessarily, because no person ever needs to be afraid of an organisation which is seeking, quite openly and in the light of the Word of God, to try to bring about the greatest good for the welfare of all the inhabitants of South Africa. [Nobody who lives in S.A. missed the implication in the last phrase.]

Two persons in particular saw his emergence as a threat to everything they promoted: one was the Rev. J. S. Gericke, the powerful dominee in the Western Cape, pastor at the time in the historic university town of Stellenbosch; the other was the brother of the next Prime Minister, the Rev. Dr. J. D. Vorster. Gericke's funeral oration at the grave of the assassinated Prime Minister, H. F. Verwoerd, September 6, 1966, is a classic in religious nationalism. Both Gericke and Verwoerd were the very backbone of the "Christian nationalism" entrenched in Stellenbosch, where Verwoerd had been a professor when Naudé was a student. Naudé's departure from his culture-religion was understood as traitorous. Gericke's eulogy, based on the text, 2 Samuel 10:12, focuses upon the cleavage developing:

Dr. Verwoerd's legacy is a determined nation. The nation has lost the man, but has retained the message of his life. If the signs are read correctly, the nation would have great need of this message in the years ahead. . . .
[And what is this central message?]
His belief that God in His wisdom had created races and racial differences so that each group could develop to the best of its ability within the confines of its own cultural tradition, was the transcending conviction of his life.

.   .   .   .   .

It is this message of the life and work of Dr. Hendrik Verwoerd which has become the enduring possession of the nation and from which we have gained so enormously.

During the ensuing years of Naudé's defection, Vorster was becoming the most powerful spokesman for the NGK, eventually becoming its Moderator. If one follows the record of attacks upon Naudé made by Vorster (cf., e.g., his 1965 statement that the CI was "a front organization for the enemies of our policy"), one can understand the childish glee of his triumph over Naudé in the government decree of June, 1975—clearly the revelation of a personal vendetta on his part. Moreover, Naudé's two declared enemies ventured to take the issue beyond the borders of South Africa by introducing their "smear" of Naudé and the Christian Institute into the proceedings of the Reformed Ecumenical Synod at Lunteren, Holland, in 1968.

Thus his official church never left off hounding Naudé. In fact, their legal case against him and the Institute, in Calvinistic canon law, drags on to this day. The 1966 General Synod of the NGK made a long condemnatory decision which practically branded the Christian Institute as a heresy. All members and ministers of the NGK were asked to withdraw from the Institute. The tragic fact at present is that no ministers of the NGK are any longer members. The continuation of this antagonism naturally bothers Naudé because he feels it is totally unjustified. He has expressed his concern poignantly:

> . . . I am convinced that in this particular case my Church has acted in conflict with the Word of God and with the precept of the Gospel, and because I work and pray and trust that my Church will see their mistake and correct it, and I do this because I have this deep and inner warm love for my Church as part of the Church of Christ in South Africa.

Needless to say, these two organizations have been the sounding board, the soapbox, for Naudé's every idea. He has never made a secret of his true opinions or intentions. They became his new pulpit. Every new social crisis would be matched by some new revelation from God. In so doing he naturally exposed himself to the criticisms of being pre-mature, too naïve, and egotistical, putting his own self above the sober, careful deliberations of the church. It cannot be denied that these organizations gave him an opportunity to run ahead of, to short-circuit, and even to contravene the usual cumbersome machinery of official Christendom, and therefore risk the danger of isolation and impracticality. But the transparency of his

motivation cannot be denied, nor his welcoming of public debate. He had to get used to finding himself in the minority when
speaking for God, and to face intense hostility. Asked in his trial,
"Have you ever flinched from this unpopularity?" Naudé answered:

> In the beginning before I joined the Christian Institute,
> yes, as I mentioned yesterday, because I realized to some
> extent what deep tensions this would bring and the rejec-
> tion, especially from the Afrikaans-speaking community,
> and that is why it took me a long time to overcome the
> anxiety and fear in the realization that if I remain true
> to the light of the Gospel, then that obedience to Christ
> would also take away all fear.

> *Interrogator:* And do you and the Christian Institute try to
> live out fearlessly the spirit and the implications (of the
> Gospel)?

> We try to do this but I have to add immediately, to
> remove any possible misunderstanding, that the impres-
> sion should not be created through my words as if the
> Christian Institute places itself above any Church in
> South Africa or any Christian or Christian group who
> does not possibly exercise this in the particular way in
> which we do it. If we do it, then we do it with a deep
> realization of our own weakness and shortcomings to be
> completely obedient, and in the application mistakes are
> certainly made due to our lack of complete insight into
> the truth of the Gospel.

This is not to say that Naudé did not entertain misgivings
about the church in general, misgivings that raised radical
doubt within his soul during the trying years of his continuing
ordeal. His faith in the church sank awfully low sometimes. At
times he appears to have no hope at all for the church. Any
ambivalence he may have had about this point seems to have
given way to radical mistrust of late.

In three major addresses within the year 1975–76, all three
published throughout the world, Naudé reiterated his despondency over the church's effectiveness. Addressing the "Christians of Europe" in the latest of these, October 31, 1976, he says:

"The institutional church in South Africa finds itself impotent because of this unresolved internal tension. Unable to speak with one voice, it is in no position to teach by example and to lead South Africa's people out of injustice and discrimination, taking the inequality out of the political system." In the Convocation Address delivered to the University of Natal in 1975, he confides, "I am therefore reluctantly forced to the conclusion that there is very little hope that the churches as institutions would be willing or able to take the lead in bringing about the fundamental change which is so desperately required to avoid a major confrontation between White and Black in our country." Lastly, there is his speech to the Royal Institute of International Affairs in London (which had to be read in absentia since Naudé could receive no passport to attend in December, 1975): "Unfortunately, I cannot share the optimistic view as to the decisions of recent synods of the three D.R.C.'s and the conservative leadership elected gives me no hope to believe that any worthwhile change could be expected from this source in time to influence white political thinking to move in the opposite direction."

Naudé was not alone in his pessimism. By 1976 most of those still expecting liberation from the official church were aware that the majority denominations of SA were of little help. Typical is this excerpt from Gatsha Buthelezi, Chief of the Zulus and a close associate of Naudé, who aroused the nation in a speech on March 14, 1976, entitled "In This Approaching Hour of Crisis." In it he called for an actual participation of all Christians who are concerned about the future. The crucial paragraph follows:

Let the Church in South Africa support the move of the majority in their movement towards constructive unity. The Church has in the past only paid lip service to this ideal. Some churches have not even done that much. Black Christians must recognize that they have to take the lead at the National level. There may be protests from some White Christians, when they hear what I have said today, about the Church, but my answer is that the Church is rapidly losing credibility among Blacks. If Churches are convinced that they have acted properly, then they have only convinced themselves. The Church has not been effective in its support for the Black liberation struggle, although outstanding individual Christians have witnessed. It is time for Black Christians to take the lead in the matter.

Yet in spite of his explicitly harsh statements on the integrity of the church, especially the Dutch Reformed, Naudé has consistently been loyal to it, being a regular communicant, establishing his message upon its foundations, and believing that its dry bones can live again. As might be expected, he has shifted more and more to the language of, and expectation of the realization of, a "confessional church." This motif appears early in his writings in *Pro Veritate* and in his expressed aspirations within the Christian Institute, but as the lines have been drawn sharper and the tension tighter, he seems to nourish himself on the possibility of its realization. In his London speech just cited, he writes:

> . . . In the meantime there is an urgent need for a confessing community to emerge from the institutionalized, organized churches in South Africa. Such a movement cannot be created or organized by human endeavor; it must be born out of the need of the situation, out of the pressures of events, out of the crisis of the hour. If effective and meaningful, however small, it will bind a number of Christians of all races and colour and social standing into a new covenant of love, taking the example of the New Testament community as a model of unity, of sharing and of service. If emerging, such a community will inevitably have to face the persecution which will follow, the suffering which will have to be endured and the sacrifices which will have to be made.

Does it follow that Naudé hates the official church?

> I do not hold anything against the Afrikaans Churches. I have something against the unbiblical points of view in our Afrikaans Churches, in which it is my calling and duty as a Christian to bring everything which, according to my conviction, is in conflict with Scriptures to the attention of our Afrikaans Churches and in particular the Church to which I belong, the NGK.

It is this gracious mood of acceptance in-spite-of and eagerness to work for reconciliation that have surely sustained Naudé over these years of persecution, when the very institution he loved the most labelled him "heretic, rebel, a thing to flout." To use his words, "I go on with my task because that is the way I see it, as I understand the Gospel, that Christ Jesus demands from you that your attitude to every man should be that of love and of forgiveness, friend or foe, that you must not allow any hatred or bitterness to enter into your heart or into your life."

CHAPTER THREE
Divine or Civil Obedience?

In 1933 Dietrich Bonhoeffer stood up publicly against the injustices of Hitler's Germany. Twelve years later, April 7, 1945, he was taken from his concentration camp cell and killed on orders from Hitler. But in between those years had come to fruition one of the greatest theologians of ethics and within the corporate life of Germany itself there was the renewal of Christianity in the Confessional Church and the Christian challenge to the super-state.

Much the same can be said with regard to the emergence of Christian Frederic Beyers Naudé within South Africa, which has come about within roughly the same time period under a government of similar racist policies. In the truest sense the "confessing church" of South Africa was born with Naudé's farewell sermon on November 3, 1963, to the Aasvoelkop Congregation in the suburbs of Johannesburg. That sermon, "Obey God Rather than Man," challenged the authority of the official church.

Naudé's challenge to the authority of the State reached its crucible on August 11, 1973, when he and four persons comprising the executive staff of the Christian Institute refused to testify before a parliamentary commission.

As followers of Christ, we accept and wish to obey Him as our highest authority, and therefore we regard any cooperation in this matter to be a betrayal of our Lord. This stand is in accord with the recent manifesto for "Christian Change" published by the Institute, which states: "Law and Government are subject to the Gospel of Christ and injustice and totalitarian activities must be rejected. Faced by unchristian laws, Christians should obey God rather than man."

This action—the advance notice to the state of the Christian conscience's refusal to cooperate with its demonic demands and the willingness to suffer the consequences—was not new for Naudé, since he had been preaching and practicing it for over a decade now. What was new was the government's apparent willingness to press for a final confrontation.* In the mounting government opposition since 1973 Naudé has had another government indictment against him, has had his passport seized, has endorsed a Council of Churches' resolution to counsel citizens against military service in behalf of what it labels "a fundamentally unjust and discriminatory society," as of May 28, 1975, has had both organs, the *Pro Veritate* journal and the Christian Institute, declared by the government to be "Affected Organizations" and therefore unable to receive supporting funds from outside the country (which in the case of the CI comprise 80% of the budget), and was banned on October 19, 1977.

What is unique about Naudé's Christian resistance to the South African government is both his timing and his ethnic background. Well known is the fact that, prior to Naudé's emergence during the previous decades, the peculiar problems of South Africa were debated vigorously, both within the country and in Britain. But the debate was lodged mostly within the liberal English-speaking element. Right at the moment of the declaration of the Republic—freedom from the British Commonwealth and the transfer of power, political, economic, and cultural, from the traditional hands of the British to the Afrikaners—there issued from the heart of Afrikaner nationalism the government's severest critic. The English-speaking liberals within the church were being silenced: Fr. Trevor Huddleston,

---

*"It is generally known that the Government is against the existence and the work of the Christian Institute. The CI witnesses in words and deeds in the name of Christ against the unchristian policy of apartheid. . . ." See Documents D–1–2–3.

(Naught for Your Comfort), in 1955, the Rev. Mr. Michael
Scott, *(A Time to Speak)*, 1957, Bishop Ambrose Reeves, 1960
(all ousted from the country), and Alan Paton *(Cry, the Beloved
Country)*, whose passport was seized in 1960. Not that voices
such as Paton, Prof. Edgar Brookes, *(The City of God and the
Politics of Crisis)*, Member of Parliament Helen Sussman, or
Prof. Monica Wilson could ever be stopped, but what was badly
needed was a protest voice within Afrikanerdom—which
Naudé supplied. Moreover, black leadership from the African
nationalist parties were equally squelched, either held in prison
on Robben Island or under house arrest like Chief Albert Luthuli, the first Black South African to receive the Nobel Peace
Prize. The hopes and fears of these transitional years have been
aptly capsuled by South Africa's best known citizen, Alan Paton,
in an essay written on his seventieth birthday: "In 1938 I was
a believer in the resurgence of Afrikanerdom. I could see good
in Afrikaner Nationalism. In 1973, I can do so no longer. Its
cruelties are insupportable."

At the very moment when it seemed to the powers-that-be
that they had everything under control, meaning the triumph
of Afrikaner messianism, meaning white dominance with rigid
apartheid and separate development under tribal homelands,
meaning "Christian nationalism," there arose a prophet from
within the House of Judah itself.

The national anthem of South Africa, referred to under the
English title, "The Call of South Africa," bespeaks the intense
messianism which Naudé is mounted against.

> *Ringing out from our blue heavens,*
> *from our deep seas breaking round;*
> *Over everlasting mountains*
> *where the echoing crags resound;*
> *From our plains where creaking wagons*
> *cut their trails into the earth—*
> *Calls the spirit of our Country,*
> *of the land that gave us birth.*

*   *   *   *   *

In Thy power, Almighty, trusting,
did our fathers build of old;
Strengthen then, O Lord, their children
to defend, to love, to hold—
That the heritage they gave us
for our children yet may be;
Bondsmen only to the Highest
and before the whole world free.
As our fathers trusted humbly,
teach us, Lord, to trust Thee still;
Guard our land and guide our people
in Thy way to do Thy will.

Naudé's movement to central stage came about unexpectedly, with almost no signals and premonitions. Yet it certainly came about propitiously—some say, providentially, for not unlike Hitler's fear of Bonhoeffer is the ruling powers' fear of Naudé. Naudé is a personified symbol of their basic and underlying fears. Fear causes whites to resort to the oppressive maintenance of white supremacy over the black majority. Fear causes most whites to support a system of oppression even though many may occasionally concede it unjust. Through the exploitation of these fears the government exercises wider control. Fear is compounded by the punitive action the government wields against any expressed opposition to its policies. By means of a massive network of informers and security agents, the government is able to intimidate those who would oppose it. The culture has become obsessed with fear: fear of overseas pressures (from sources such as the United Nations, the World Council of Churches, and even multinational investors), fear of Communist subversives and guerilla infiltrators, fear of Black African liberation forces on their borders, and fear of intellectual enquiry and dialogue.

Naudé and the ecumenical and interracial voice that centers in the Christian Institute would expose these fears, finding them exaggerated, distorted or unfounded. Replacing this climate of fear with the extended hand of brotherhood, with the positive method of non-violence, and with the openness of trust and love, Naudé would release the creative potential of this richly endowed country with its promising peoples. Thus Naudé serves two roles in the present South Africa. On the one hand, he is the focused victim of the climate of fear; on the other hand, he is the victor, and the symbol of victory over these fears. In this sense, Naudé is a harbinger of what all South Africans could become. His kind is South Africa's finest product.

Naudé's pilgrimage toward liberation theology over the past fifteen years has taught him that release from fear to creative relationships is not easy. That he perceptively envisioned the present crisis is clear upon rereading his editorial messages contained in the Christian Institute newsletters. Typical is this one of March, 1969:

THE CHOICE IS IMMINENT!

It must be clear to anyone who reads this Newsletter with any measure of attention that the Christian Institute finds itself involved in all kinds of turmoil from the very outset this year.

That this is the case is a sign of healthy life for which we are deeply grateful. It also provides a clear answer to the question of some: does the Institute still have any real purpose and significance and is it still achieving anything effective?

At a far deeper level, however, it points towards an unmistakable development in the life of the Church of Christ in South Africa. Things are gradually, but ever more swiftly, moving to a head, to a moment of choice and decision for every Christian. This is, of course, largely due to the "Message to the People of South Africa" and its still echoing repercussions. A confrontation is taking place between essentially irreconcilable forces which is already leaving no confessing Christian and his conscience untouched and will increasingly do so. The time of decision is coming closer for all of us. A clear choice will have to be effected and everyone will have to decide before God where he stands. What we so piously confess is being progressively put to the proof of practice and harsh reality.

We can only thank the Lord for our imminent extrication from the deadlock in which we have been bogged down for so many years, and also for the very real role which the Christian Institute has been playing in the attainment of this eve-of-battle situation. May He bring more and more of our members to a realisation of the urgency of our calling and responsibility.

(Significantly, the Le Grange Commission Report #6 focused on "The Message," cited by Naudé in this editorial, as most objectionable to the government.)

That his witness will continue, no doubt even more aggravatingly to the state, follows from his announcement in the face of the May, 1975, government curtailment of the CI. "I believe," he said, "local support will enable us to continue, though on a much more limited scale. We can function effectively on a budget of R2,000,000 a year.* Even if this is cut by half we shall be able to continue with the major part of our work." (For a man who began on a shoestring and an uphill climb, he exaggerates his needs!) His most reliable income is the solid wealth of support from a vocal minority of prominent South African Christians. The South African Council of Churches issued a statement in his behalf as did the Catholic Bishops. In part the SACC statement reads: "We express our support and prayer for the director of the C.I., Dr. Beyers Naudé, who has been subject to the most vicious attack in the Commission's report. We question his being singled out for these attacks, when he is simply representing the views of a strong segment of Christians in S.A. We believe however, that to be attacked by this Commission can only add to Dr. Naude's stature." The Bishops declared, "Dr. Naudé and the C.I. stand for a South Africa of radical change from the apartheid-separate development image and are striving to save the country from violence. . . . Without radical change no detente is possible, only violence."

The lead editorial in the June, 1975, issue of *Pro Veritate*

---

*In late 1977 the value of the South African Rand was 1.15 American dollars.

signifies the new stage of confrontation: the powerless and the
limited before the Pilate of power unlimited.

> The first thing the C.I. must realize is that in this situation it
> has but *little power*. The government has not based its
> authority on *right* or justice or on Christian principles, but
> on the power of violence which it wields arbitrarily.... This
> position of little power—as regards financial measures also
> —is however in accord with the gospel of Jesus Christ....
> The C.I. will if possible go forward in the Name of the Lord
> —and this depends largely on your support and that of
> others—but the question now is what will the church in
> general in S. A. do? Will it permit the present violent system
> to develop into a possible blood-bath or will it commit itself
> completely to Christian radical change on a non-violent
> basis even if this brings about suffering?

Thus, from the very outset, Naudé was painfully conscious
of being a marked man. The years 1963 and 1964 confirmed his
worst fears. The intense opposition of the state accompanied
the favored attention he received from foreign critics of South
Africa and the growing number of Africans within his own
nation who found in Naudé their best hope for liberation. But
the crowning affront to the ruling powers was Naudé's resignation from the Broederbond and the peculiar circumstances surrounding that exposure.

Naudé has never ceased to be apologetic about these circumstances, apologetic both to his friends who sympathized
and to the members of the Broederbond, his former friends
under a secret oath. Yes, even to them. The full details of this
awkward affair have never been chronicled. But this is how
Naudé referred to what happened in his trial:

> In 1963, as a result of long and painful struggling in my own
> conscience for more than a year previously, I decided to
> resign and my objection was based mainly on two aspects,
> first the principle of secrecy of the Broederbond and se-
> condly my objection that the Broederbond by means of
> circulars and otherwise influenced, exercised unwarranted
> influence in the discussion and in the decisions of the
> Church.

About this time he composed a letter to the Broederbond stating his intentions to resign. Apparently all this was to be done without public ado. One must remember that this was in the formative years when Naudé had not fully committed himself to a radical course of action. In any case, what ensued remained an embarassment to Naudé forever afterwards. To continue from his testimony:

> The way in which the whole matter progressed, the fact that before my decision and as a result of my earnest struggle and unclarity about it I took some of these documents and gave them to Professor Geyser, that it appeared in the press caused me much grief, personal grief in my life. I also know that it caused much sorrow to the members of the Afrikaner Broederbond. I have already apologized on more than one occasion, in public offered my apology for that grief which I caused to the members of the Broederbond, and if it is [now] necessary I do it again.

Apparently what happened is that a certain theological professor, Dr. A. S. Geyser, who was under fire from his own branch of the Dutch Reformed Church, called upon Naudé for some help in his own defense. The anxious conversation of both parties must have focused on the seriousness of the issue, and Naudé, who at the moment had some of these secret Broederbond circulars within his possession, trustingly turned them over to Professor Geyser. Within a day or so their contents were spread across the pages of the daily papers. A certain journalist, Charles Bloomberg, had been trying for years to expose the Broederbond, and it seems that as soon as these papers under Naudé's care fell into Geyser's hands they were turned over to Bloomberg. Needless to say, what caused jubilation among the liberals amounted to consternation among the Afrikaners. Many of the Afrikaner Christians inclined to sympathize with Naudé and who might have followed him at a distance were offended by what they took to be Naude's underhanded dealings. They could not believe a man of his noble intentions and high position could stoop so low—not that he had just broken

his vows, but the devious way he had apparently done so. There
was certainly no heroism in the act, even for Naudé.

To continue with his clarification of the matter from the
trial:

> The manner in which it was made known, or rather the
> factors that went with it, were in my opinion not in agree-
> ment with the light which God wanted to give me and
> which at that time I was not mature enough, open enough
> to receive. This brought me to the conclusion that through
> the grace of God I should try for the rest of my life to do
> everything in the open and in public.

The same year, 1964, a small group of ministers from the
African Independent Churches approached Naudé for assistance in their development. Responding positively, a conference was called and the following resolution was passed: "We
give this day full trust in God and His People, that we must love
each other as brothers in Christ irrespective of colour, race or
creed and to share together those sufferings which He shed on
the Cross, with other nations. We give our fullest confidence to
the Christian Institute of Southern Africa, and invite its Director, the Rev. C. F. B. Naudé, to guide us through every difficulty
in the Christian field." From that modest beginning, leaning
heavily upon Naudé, was born one more powerful force in
opposition to the ruling power of South Africa. The Association
of African Independent Churches was provided a staff member
by the CI, the Rev. Danie van Zyl, and it grew beyond the
wildest dreams, finally becoming altogether self-reliant in 1973.
Four years after the founding of AICA, the wives of the clergy
decided that they would like to establish their own association,
the Women's Association of the African Independent Churches,
and to have their own office and staff. Once again the CI came
to their aid, posing another potential counter-force to the government.

Also in 1964 the British Council of Churches issued their
severe indictment of S.A. policies and urged such recommendations upon Christians as the refusal to invest capital in that
country. The time and the headaches which consumed Naudé

in meeting with and interpreting such armchair critics from abroad is hard to imagine for a person unfamiliar with the situation. It became a tightrope act for Naudé. He was exposed on all sides, for he was obliged to interpret sympathetically the motives and the specifics of the critics to his homeland, and the subtleties and the multifarious complexity of his compatriots' reservations to the document to the daily stream of visiting critics. He had to make clear his disagreement and consensus with both sides. Fortunately he was blessed with the ingenuity to rise above the doctrinaire position of both. Yet he was doomed to be misunderstood by all parties, making his newly assumed role virtually impossible. A year after the issuance of the BCC report, *Pro Veritate* was still struggling to establish what was valid and what was useful in it for the South African situation.

Thus from the year of the establishment of the Christian Institute Naudé's role in S.A. was fixed. Catapulted into a position of leadership he had neither sought nor expected, it is not surprising that his opposition grew bolder—and in certain of their naïve procedures actually strengthened his hand. He is attacked by broadcasts on the government-controlled radio, his house and office is searched in May, 1965, by the secret police, and in November he is deprived of his status as clergyman by the DNG Synod. Probably the most frightening conspiracy against him, though, were the widespread charges that he was a Communist or "fronting" for Communism. (We have already mentioned the Moderator of the Cape Synod's accusation on that point.) What was so frightening is that in the McCarthy-like hysteria of South Africa a court action proving a citizen to be a member of the Communist party might carry a death penalty.

Within that atmosphere a certain professor, Dr. A. D. Pont, wrote a series of articles in which Naudé and one of the CI Board members were so accused. Naturally the wording was such that the ambiguity of it might avoid a libel suit. Still, in an unheard-of action, Naudé and his colleague sued Professor Pont for damages, and in a trial that focused world attention upon South Africa's judicial system risked their very lives and careers

—for not to win was suicide. Churchmen from all over the world took notice and thousands of dollars were collected in Europe and Britain and the United States for litigation on behalf of Naudé. Proceedings were initiated in 1966; the trial itself actually began on February 15, 1967; it was finally resolved in 1968, surprisingly to the advantage of Naudé and colleague.

Nonetheless, while under the very weight of this tension, in October, 1965, Naudé and three other Afrikaner theologians of the CI sent a letter to the 1,500 ministers of the NGK warning that a strong political current was pushing S.A. "in the direction of making the political ideology of apartheid the highest authority over the consciences of the people, elevating it above the Word of God as the yardstick of the Christian faith." "Try the Spirits" is the title of their open letter, and it ranks as a classic in the Christian enterprise of exposing the false gospels of this world, "the work of the devil" as they call it. "Is there not a hand of the Devil stretched out towards our Christian freedom, towards the freedom of our conscience, our worship and our witness? Is it not hate of Christ and His Gospel which is busy manifesting itself out of passionate religious worship of natural gods such as race, land, blood, culture?"

As we have seen, the answer of the official church to this appeal was the rejection of the Christian Institute as a "heretical church," enacted by the NGK in the fall of 1966. Nonetheless, the actual adjudication was to drag on for over a decade—testifying not only to the niceties of Calvinistic canon law but also to the doubts of many church law interpreters as to the propriety of such an action against Naudé and to the influence of other learned and prominent NGK clergymen who had joined his cause. While he had lost many of the fainthearted and sunshine patriots, he had gathered to his witness a few stalwarts within his own denomination as well as some recognition in the country at large.

Naturally, with increased world attention focused upon Naudé, he was becoming the central figure to consult on the white side in the movement to liberate Africa. Even so, black African liberation feelings and forces were moving faster than

Naudé and world Christian considerations. This growing cleavage may be traced in the periodic sessions of the All-Africa Church Conference (which came into being in the very years of Naudé's emergence), in its various consultations in cooperation with the World Council, and in the Mindola Ecumenical Centre for all of Africa located in Zambia. In the founding of the AACC Alan Paton and other South Africans had been major contributors; in fact, Dr. Donald M'Timkulu was chosen as its first full-time Secretary. However, in the rapid-fire alterations in race relations the world over, it soon became impossible for whites to retain the easy-going mixture of the initial years or to exercise any major office in its affairs. Moreover, pressure from the government was placed upon both white and black participants from South Africa to refrain from entering into the enthusiasm of the black liberation theology more and more expressive of the AACC.

Nevertheless, Naudé continued to find himself in the middle of black African ferment as articulated by the meetings referred to and the growing concern of the World Council of Churches about this region. Therefore in the preliminaries leading up the latter's assembly held at Uppsala in 1968, Naudé's influence was considerable, and he was present for the Uppsala sessions. (Significantly, the subsequent WCC conference, the Fifth Assembly, convened for the first time on African soil, in Nairobi, in 1975.) Its most debatable action was the establishment of funds for the support of the newly created Program to Combat Racism (PCR), much of which were devoted to the liberation forces in southern Africa. This gave rise to an even more vicious attack upon Naudé, especially in the light of the question of whether a Christian might use violence in the promotion of human liberation. The PCR, despite the fact that it laid down stipulations that the liberation forces were to use their funds only for medical, food, and educational purposes, was considered to be endorsing violence.

Naudé took great pains to dissociate himself from any taint of a Christian using violence, a position he had maintained from the very beginning of his radical change and a principle he was

forced more and more to expound in all its complexity within
the increasingly inflammatory climate of South Africa. Increasingly the columns of *Pro Veritate* and the editorials of the CI
newsletters were devoted to this matter; he and his associates
even developed specific working papers on the subject. Everywhere he staunchly reiterated his absolute pacifist stand.

Naudé's dilemma is nowhere better expressed than in his
Director's Report to the CI in June, 1969:

> In the past two years, partly because of the increase in
> strength and influence of the militant Black Power and
> anti-apartheid groups throughout the Western world also
> in ecumenical affairs, the feeling against Southern Africa,
> because of our racist policies, has been steadily mounting,
> and calls for violent action have been made from within
> Christian groups. . . . The task of the Christian has thus
> become a very difficult one. On the one hand the CI has
> stated unequivocally that it is against violence as a solution
> of our race problem; on the other hand it cannot but give
> its full support to the cry for justice and do everything in
> its power as a body of deeply concerned Christians to trans-
> form attitudes, customs and policies which could lead to
> serious and possibly uncontrollable outbursts of violence.
> And yet our path is clear: despite criticism from some over-
> seas groups of our being too conservative (and exactly the
> opposite indictment from many whites in South Africa of
> our being far too radical) we will have to pursue the course
> of obedience to God and His Word as we understand it
> through Christ.

The razor's edge which Naudé was forced to walk became
even more torturous. Before his compatriots he was obliged to
defend and to explain the PCR policies; before the rabid endorsement of liberation-violence by certain Christian world-
leaders he was obliged to disown the support of violence by
Christians. (For example, Bishop Edward Crowther, an American who had been deported from South Africa in 1965 and now
as Bishop in California was saying in 1972: "The time has gone,
if indeed it ever existed, when merely verbal statements from
religious leaders deploring the evils of racism in Southern
Africa are sufficient. I believe that the power of the churches

must be employed in the support of movements of liberation now struggling for freedom in Southern Africa.")

Like King in America, he could fall back upon the Gandhi interpretation of the power of non-violence. This had a more authentic appeal in his country, because Gandhi as a young lawyer out of Britain had begun his method in South Africa, and the spiritual community he established outside Durban called "Phoenix" still existed, though in a bedraggled state. Nonetheless, in the refinement of the use of violence on the part of Christians, Naudé ran into two encroachments: one from the alarm on the part of his countrymen about the rapid success of black liberation on its frontiers and the other from the black liberation forces' leaders, many of whom were Christian and who insisted that just as Americans had used armed force in their revolution and South Africans had used armed force in their political history, so might present-day Africans. What began with the establishment of the PCR came to a head in the Lusaka meeting of the All-Africa Church Conference in May, 1974.

In response to the Uppsala Assembly's Martin Luther King resolution (1968), and the controversy provoked by the World Council of Churches' humanitarian aid to the groups combatting racism (1970), the W.C.C. Central Committee (Addis Ababa, 1971) had asked its sub-unit on Church and Society to conduct a two-year study on the problems and potentialities of violence and non-violence in the struggle for social justice. This study was promulgated in August, 1973. What this study theorized, the Third Assembly of the All-Africa Conference of Churches meeting in Lusaka in May, 1974, concretized. Zambia's President Kenneth Kaunda, himself a strong Christian and writer of several books on Christianity and politics, in the opening address identified himself with the liberation struggle: "Liberation Movements are helping to create the conditions in which the aspirations expressed in the Christian Gospel can be fulfilled." The Assembly's leader, a priest, Canon Burgess Carr, brought the matter into the open in his secretarial address: "If for no other reason, we must give our unequivocal support to

the Liberation Movements, because they helped the Church to
rediscover a new and radical appreciation of the Cross. In accepting the violence of the Cross, God, in Jesus Christ, sanc-
tified violence into a redemptive instrument for bringing into
being a fuller human life."

In aligning himself unequivocally with non-violence, Naudé
was simply stating his way of settling the South African crisis—
what had been his theme from his very first emergence on the
political scene in the early 1960's, reiterated repeatedly, right
up through his Chicago speech of December, 1974. His editorial in the first year of *Pro Veritate* could very well be reprinted
today:

> Times of crisis are times of testing for the Church and for
> Christians. The test is basically one of loyalty and witness
> —loyalty to Christ and witness to his Kingship. On the face
> of it the crisis may seem to have nothing to do with Christ
> and our Christian belief—but eventually it becomes clear
> that the issues at stake are not primarily political or eco-
> nomic or educational or social but theological and moral.
> We are living in such times in Africa—and especially in the
> southern part of this continent. On the face of it the clash
> between groups is an ideological one being waged on the
> political and the economic level. But God sees it differ-
> ently. . . . This has a special significance for South Africa
> because recent developments give the impression as if the
> tension and possible clash may become one between black
> and white. Therefore Christians, white and non-white,
> must be led to understand that their first allegiance, their
> primary loyalty, is to Christ and to his Kingdom, to his
> Person as the only Truth—and that all other loyalties are
> secondary. (April 15, 1963)

In his acceptance speech, upon the occasion of the Niebuhr
Award at the University of Chicago in 1974, he focuses on the
issue of non-violent change:

> This is one of the crucial questions with which the Christian
> Church and the Christian community throughout the
> world is faced, together with all the inhabitants of the
> globe. Deep differences of conviction are being held and
> expressed on this issue not only within but also outside the

organized Church. I do not think that Christ gives us the right to judge or condemn those who, in finding themselves in such situations of tyranny and oppression, have come to the conclusion that, having tried all else, there is no option left to procure liberation but through violence. But I hold the conviction that this is not, cannot be, and will never be the truly satisfying answer which God has made available to his children on earth.

We are committed, in accordance with our understanding of the Christian faith, to do everything in our power to achieve these goals by peaceful means; we are committed to the task of reconciliation based on justice and of Christian liberation through justice without which no lasting reconciliation could be procured.

It goes without saying that his countrymen would be divided in their opinions about Naudé's position, some who, self-serving, would stoop to distort his actual position. The Le Grange Commission Report issued on Naudé and the Christian Institute in May, 1975, called it "a danger to the State," charged it guilty of advocating violence, and held that it "aims at a black-dominated socialist state and accepts violence as an element in achieving it, and that its strategy is characteristic of revolutionary socialist techniques." The defense for Naudé rallied in the form of the Catholic Bishops, the Anglican Bishops, the President of the Methodist Church, the Executive Committee of the Federation of Evangelical Lutheran Church, the Presbyterians, the United Church, and others. All cited Naudé's stress on *peaceful* change. In fact, they supported him as the major possibility of hope for peaceful change. The Lutherans declared, "These churches, like ourselves, are committed to *peaceful* change, and it is a gross distortion of facts to argue otherwise." The Anglican Archbishop of Capetown agreed: "We for our part will, of course, continue to support projects of the Christian Institute as in the past and seek to encourage such changes in the social order by which alone *peace* can be assured in South Africa." Owen Cardinal McCann wrote that the CI "stands for the same social teachings as the Catholic Church."

As if this were not enough heat, Naudé and the Christian

Institute initiated during this time, actually in 1969, a scholarly investigation of the influence of apartheid upon the South Africa society, The Study Project on Christianity in Apartheid Society. From the very outset, its purposes were so ambitious and its scholars so knowledgeable that it was obliged to establish itself as a separate adjunct to the CI and develop its own press. Over the next five years its exposures were of such monumental import that each of its books was subject to government scorn, several being banned altogether, down to the final summary volume, *A Taste of Power,* banned in November, 1973. By March, 1974, five had "succeeded" in being banned. Quite logically many of its staff and contributors were also harassed and finally indicted. The CI, in setting up this group, known henceforth by its acronym, SPRO-CAS, was able to secure the brilliant editorship of Peter Randall, later to stand alongside Naudé in his trials.

Meanwhile Naudé had stepped into more "hot water" by sponsoring along with the South African Council of Churches (which CI had spurred from a generally inofficious bureaucracy in the early 60's to a heroic companion witness by the 70's) "A Message to the People of South Africa," 1968. This document is crucial because it occasions the first general church endorsement of Naudé's principles and position. It serves as a Barmen Manifesto to South Africa. Following Naudé, it begins by pitting the "Gospel of Jesus Christ" against the false gospel:

> Therefore, we believe that the Church must enable all our people to distinguish between this false, novel gospel and the true eternal gospel of Jesus Christ. We believe that it is the Church's duty to enable our people to discriminate more carefully between what may be demanded of them as subjects or citizens of the State of South Africa and what is demanded of them as disciples of Jesus Christ.

Next, it attacks head on the policy of apartheid or separate development:

> The policy of separate development does not take proper account of these truths. It promises peace and harmony between the people of our country not by a faithful and

obedient pursuit of the reconciliation wrought by Christ, but through separation, which, being precisely the opposite course, is a demonstration of unbelief and distrust in the power of the Gospel.

This amounts to a denial of the central statements of the Gospel. It is opposed to the Christian understanding of the nature of man and community. It, in practice, severely restricts the ability of Christian brothers to serve and know each other, and even to give each other simple hospitality. It arbitrarily limits the ability of a person to obey the Gospel's command to love his neighbour as himself.

Any demonstration of the reality of reconciliation would endanger this policy; therefore the advocates of this policy inevitably find themselves opposed to the Church if it seeks to live according to the Gospel and if it shows that God's grace has overcome our hostilities. A thorough policy of racial separation must ultimately require that the Church should cease to be the Church.

We believe that we are under an obligation to state that our country and Church are under God's judgement, and that Christ is inevitably, a threat to much that is called 'the South African way of life.' We must ask ourselves what features of our social order will have to pass away if the lordship of Christ is to be fully acknowledged and if the peace of God is to be revealed as the destroyer of our fear.

Then comes the most telling harbinger of what was to come for Christians who aligned themselves with this manifesto:

We confess, therefore, that we are under an obligation to live in accordance with the Christian understanding of man and of community, *even if this be contrary to some of the customs and laws of this country.* [Italics added]

Needless to say, the main body of Christians in South Africa, the three Dutch Reformed churches who had long since withdrawn from the Council of Churches, did not go along with the manifesto, and as was expected sought every way to discredit it. However, the Roman Catholic House of Bishops in South Africa came out strongly in favor of it, and even went further by formulating their own, "A Call to Conscience," in the spring of 1972. Though belated, it was supportive, because the public debate over the manifesto continues to this day.

With the beginning of the 70's the thunder and lightning of the gathering storm began to strike all around Naudé, taking its toll of his friends and staff. Already in 1968 the passport of the Rev. Basil Moore, of the University Christian Movement, had been taken. In 1969 the Rev. D. W. Wessels, an original board member of the CI, was banned. Thereafter the blows were in rapid-fire succession: for instance, in 1971 Fr. Cosmas Desmond, a Fransciscan on the CI staff, had his passport application refused and was later banned and house-arrested; Fr. Colin Davison, staff, was deported; Fr. Mark Collier, staff, had his passport confiscated; the CI headquarters in Capetown were raided; Dr. Francis Wilson, Member of the Board of Management of the CI, had his home raided. So it continues in a frightening crescendo in the late 70's.

Such government oppression was not unexpected or uninvited. The decade had begun with a broadside directed to the voters of South Africa (with the general election pending) published January 15, 1970. Known as the "Twelve Statements," and sponsored by Naudé among many other signees, points #9, #10, and #11 came down hard on the ruling party:

> TRUTH. In obedience to God, no Christian can support a political policy which, being demonstrably impracticable, bases its appeal to the electorate on false claims and promises. Such an essentially dishonest policy cannot be reconciled with the Christian's commitment to the truth.
> JUSTICE. In obedience to God, no Christian can support a political policy which, for its practical implementation, unavoidably necessitates open or concealed injustice towards any individual or population group. . . .
> LOVE. In obedience to God, no Christian can support a political policy which is essentially based on group selfishness and the furtherance of sectional interests only. Such a policy leads to inhumanity and lovelessness and must consequently clash with the law of love given by Christ.

With the Nationalist Party winning a resounding vote, it was just a matter of time as to when they would strike next. Perhaps they would have strategically ignored Naudé and the minority of Christians he represented, preferring like an elephant not to exhaust its energies swatting flies, had he not persisted in promoting and publishing the dissident voices breaking forth from other sources: voices from black consciousness and the black theology, voices from the students and from youths, voices from the new autonomy of the Bantustans and the liberation forces on the border of South Africa. Keeping these placed before the Christian community and even identifying with all those political prisoners who had been put away by the state was dramatically incendiary. His journal and his newsletter published regularly a "box score" so that the public could not forget. Under the heading, "Christian Solidarity with the Banned," Naudé made the following appeal during the Christmas season, 1973:

> If there is one period during the year when every human being longs to share the fellowship and the warmth of social contact within the circle of family and friends, it is during Christmas and the New Year. For one group of persons in our country this deeply needed experience is unfortunately withheld and denied: the banned. The loneliness of banning itself is a terrible reality which those who are faced with such arbitrary actions are experiencing from day to day. . . . No civilized person, least of all a Christian could ever approve or support the inhumanity of such a system and yet it not only continues but the number of persons who have been silenced and sentenced with a form of solitary confinement—and all this happening in a country proudly proclaiming itself to be Christian—is a tragic reflection of the kind of Christianity which we subscribe to and practice in this country. [Naude concludes as follows:] Therefore it is incumbent upon the CI to procure and offer wherever possible the pastoral fellowship and financial assistance to all such victims as a valid expression of our Christian concern and compassion.

The resulting polarization set the stage for the forming of the Schlebusch Commission by Parliament in 1972 (later known as the Le Grange Commission when Mr. Louis Le Grange took over its chairmanship after Mr. Alwyn Schlebusch became Speaker of the House).

Specifically brought into being to investigate the activities of four anti-apartheid organizations—the National Union of South African Students, the Institute of Race Relations, the Christian Institute and the University Christian Movement—the assignment of the Commission and its proposed methods were challengeable from the beginning. However, after watching the treatment of NUSAS and the Wilgespruit personnel before the hearings and seeing the prejudicial findings (both hit with bannings), Naudé, with the members of the executive staff and the Board of Management, issued a statement in March, 1973, in which they declared their readiness to refuse, at the risk of heavy fines or jail sentences, to give evidence before the Commission or to cooperate in its inquiry in any way. The fourth paragraph in that statement reads:

> That while we confidently affirm that we have nothing to hide, we also affirm that there is much to preserve by way of our Christian heritage of fairness and the evidencing of justice, which such a Parliamentary Commission palpably erodes.

Instead, they urged a judicial inquiry. In August they repeated this plea with the following broadside in a CI newsletter:

> The CI has, in vain, persistently asked the legislature to respect the due processes of law by appointing a Judicial Commission. Words having failed, those who seek to follow the biblical tradition of the prophet are perhaps obliged to embrace the discipline of symbolic action. Perhaps it is necessary that some of our staff risk imprisonment so that John Citizen might ask: "Has it come to this?"

On August 11 the five top staff members of CI submitted their final statement of refusal to testify to the Commission; Naudé's signature, as Director, led the list. It opens with the line:

> As followers of Christ, we accept and wish to obey Him as our highest authority, and therefore we regard any cooperation in this matter to be a betrayal of our Lord. This stand is in accord with the recent manifesto for "Christian Change" published by the Institute, which states: "Law and Government are subject to the Gospel of Christ and injustice and totalitarian activities must be rejected. Faced

by unchristian laws, Christians should obey God rather than man."

It closes as follows:

We call upon all lovers of truth and righteousness to oppose all that which frustrates God's will within our nation. For righteousness and truth alone exalt a nation.

The "manifesto" to which this statement refers is one of a three-part clarification of the Christian Institute's principles and program which they published in the summer of 1973, largely to fortify against this new challenge. Naudé quotes Number Five of an eight-point sheet entitled "Christian Change." The second brochure, "A Programme of Action," holds that "the C.I. is dedicated to help bring change in Southern Africa in the name of Christ. . . . This means seeking fundamental change in the attitudes of people, in the structures of power, and in the processes of decision-making." The "Christian Principles" brochure is slightly more expanded, and lays a theological basis for the other two. However, it is hard-hitting in that it compares side-by-side the Christian way with the South African way.

South Africa is a sick society because of its alienation and doomed to die unless it is healed. . . . The South African system perpetuates poverty, exploitation, rejection, and deprivation. . . . The South African social structures incorporate many injustices which prevent the inhabitants from realising the way of Christ. Christians are called to obey God rather than men, even if this involves disobedience to the civil authorities, passive resistance, or defying unchristian laws, and even if the solutions which they suggest are unpopular. . . . Christians who respond to God's call know that they are called to take up a cross to follow Him. The present South African system can only be maintained by the force of structured violence in opposition to God's way. It invites and is threatened by revolutionary violence. Christian change means a rapid and radical peaceful change towards a society based on the way of Christ: love, justice, freedom, truth and responsibility. Christians should expect to suffer. . . .

One notices not only the same themes stressed previously by Naudé (the evil of apartheid, the necessity of civil disobedience, the readiness to suffer, and above all the insistence on non-violence), but also how much stronger and more carefully delineated this position-paper is over the original constitution of the CI ten years previous.

It goes without saying that by now Naudé was fully prepared to back these brave words with action. On November 13, 1973, his trial commenced in the Pretoria Regional Court. What was to become a celebrated trial, whose every detail was scrutinized at home and abroad (the International Commission of Jurists had observers and afterwards published an abbreviated transcript of the proceedings), began most inauspiciously. On a day in September Naudé, called before the session of the Schlebusch Commission, had been asked to take the oath preparatory to answering questions. Naudé refused, and that was an offense under Section 6 of the Commissions Act of 1947. His defense admitted the violation of the law but held that the refusal was justified on grounds of conscience and the secrecy of the Commission's proceedings.

Thus was joined the issue of the ages: the principles of the gospel, the position of the church in S.A., the powers of the state and the limits of law, all issues of monumental, universal and lasting importance—in other words, the individual conscience versus the state.

From Naudé's side it was long in coming but expected. And ironically it provided his Christian witnessing with a public forum unavailable otherwise. From the government's side it was reluctantly enjoined since it could be interpreted as putting South Africa in a bad light. Thus, paradoxically, the trial designed by the government to curb Naudé actually did more to air his views than any other act of his life. Incorporated into the record were all the documents integral to the development of Naudé's conscience: his Aasvoelkop sermon, the Resolutions of Cottesloe, the Christian Institute's non-violent statements, the position of the church on race relations, churches from home and abroad, and significantly a newly produced document entitled "Divine or Civil Obedience?" These were all included in the testimony word for word, and of course reported in the daily papers. All South Africa was to view itself in the mirror of Naudé's trial.

Naudé was obliged, like other great persons of the twentieth century up against the state, persons such as Gandhi, King, Bonhoeffer, and Berrigan, to spell out carefully the difference between ordinary criminal disobedience to the law and the disobedience of the higher conscience. In the trial he explicated this difference as follows:

> That is why I wish to say that in any public criminal trial, if I or any other member of the Christian Institute should be charged for any action or any charge of breaking the law, we would naturally with the high regard which we have for the whole structure of law and for the process of law in our country, we would freely submit ourselves to it and should we be found guilty . . . I would accept that sentence and endure it.

* * * *

> It remains the duty, however, the right and the duty of the Christian, if he is convinced that those emergency measures are in conflict with his conscience and his point of view of the right of the authorities, to protest against it, and if it is necessary, to make it clear that he cannot go along with it, naturally with the realization of the consequences.

The government defended its position by holding that any and all laws are to be obeyed by everyone regardless of circumstances and motivation. Moreover, it justified any extreme and unusual nature of its present laws on the emergency: that "we are living in the times we live in—that such circumstances do occur and the Government by necessity must take certain action based on certain information. . . . It can happen in the best democratic systems that certain measures are taken which give the Executive wider powers to resist the situation. . . . It is surely not only the proper right but also the responsibility of a responsible government to take within the framework of its mandate to maintain law and order in the troubled world situation, even if in the process some toes are trodden on."

Thus the government sought to rest its case on the absolute

right of the state to maintain order. Naudé countered, "Provided the order is based on justice, because where order is not joined with justice then it ends in chaos." His rationale was fully ventilated in the trial, but the crux of his answer appeared as follows:

By the Court: But does this mean the overthrow of a State?

Naudé: That depends, Your Worship, what you mean by overthrow.

Court: You should possibly expand somewhat on that answer?

Naudé: The Church and the Christian have the calling to obey authority which is not in conflict with the truth of the Gospel, and to follow all the legitimate ways and means to bring this conviction to the attention of the authority to accept it. According to my point of view the Church and the Christian do not have the right to try to achieve this by means of physical violence, but by means of proclamation, of persuasion, and if a situation should arise where a Christian on the grounds of his convictions from God's word and his conscience has to disobey the law of the land, he has before God the right to disobey the law provided he understands clearly that he must then accept the results of his disobedience and endure them.

His defense counsel rested its case on the government's over-extension of powers in the functioning of the Commission, particularly on the Commission's judgments concluded in secret. Naudé pled for a public disclosure of all indictments against those accused by the government to be its enemies. Naudé declared:

I emphasize this because it is of basic importance to realize that the Church of Jesus Christ has received a commission and a message to proclaim in public. It is part of the essence of the Church that all that the Church is and proclaims should happen in public. . . . Christ himself said, "I am the light of the world."

At issue in the trial was the age-old problem involving difficult decisions for persons unable in conscience to obey what
they considered unethical demands by their government. A
government commission was suspect in its very conception if it
were obliged to investigate a school of thought or a spiritual
trend, people's ideas, and to sit in secret. The secrecy, the con-
spiratorial nature of the government's action against certain of
its citizens working for the liberation of all, was in fact on trial.

In spite of the court's high opinion of Naudé, doubtless influenced by the forthrightness and integrity of his testimony, in
every case heavily buttressed by his knowledge of the Bible and
the documents of the church, the court found him guilty and
sentenced him to a fine of 50 Rand. (Naudé appealed, but on
December 2, 1974, a higher court rejected this and he remains
under conviction, still appealing.)

The key item supporting Naudé's testimony was introduced
during the trial as "Exhibit E." It was the theological position
paper developed by Naudé and the other four staff members of
the CI in the process of their deciding not to testify. From the
day of February 27, 1973, when the Commission released its
report on the student dissidents, Naudé knew within his soul he
would be obliged to take a stand against the state.

> That night after I received the news, I reflected on it at
> length and earnestly. Early next morning I got up and
> during my quiet time I considered the matter at length and
> carefully, read portions from scriptures, and came to the
> conclusion that I could no longer see my way open for any
> co-operation with this Commission.

Exhibit E (later circulated widely as a pamphlet) is in the
classic tradition of the "here I stand" brief. It searches the
Scriptures and the classic theologians for justification of their
defiance. Significantly it draws upon the very Calvinism of
South Africa's so-called Christian Nationalism to underwrite
resistance to the government.

> The believer in Christ not only has the right, but the
> responsibility to hearken to the Word of God and His righ-
> teousness rather than to the government, should the gov-
> ernment deviate from God's will. . . . Civil disobedience is

an act of protest by the Christian on the grounds of Christian conscience. . . . Authority is only legitimate when it does not act contrary to God's will. . . . Where such deviation from the Gospel occurs, it is therefore not only the right of the Christian to resist authority, but his duty to offer passive resistance in obedience to the Gospel, even if in so doing he has to disobey the Government. . . . The Government is God's servant and this means that it cannot arbitrarily place itself above the rule of law without impinging on the highest authority. If it does, it becomes the evil-doer, which must be resisted in obedience to God.

At the end they all signed in large Hancocks, concluding, The signatories wish to remain faithful to Christ, by the grace of God because:

VERBUM DEI MANET IN AETERNUM.

CHAPTER FOUR
The Day Before the Last

June 16, 1976: the Soweto protest of schoolchildren and the subsequent police shootings, killing hundreds of youth in their puberty and adolescence. Just how and why is not certain, but the demonstration turned into days of riots, and the riots have spread over South Africa. The forced learning of the Afrikaans language was the express reason, but the deep cause was not Afrikaans. It is the pent-up hatred against the discriminatory laws and the cruelty of their enforcement.

Perhaps the time of reckoning had come. Naudé, since his trial, had become increasingly gloomy about the prospects of the ruling powers changing in order to avoid the bloodbath which he had worried about so long. He now began to speculate publicly about the "war psychosis" of his countrymen. He perceived the government's move in the Schlebusch Commission to be an irreversible step in the direction of tyranny. He held that "the Government has introduced a strain of lawlessness into public affairs, [and] contributed to a progressive erosion of respect for law and order." Again he wrote, "Have we come to this pass that we can no longer be governed save by abominations peculiar to communistic and totalitarian lands such as state witch-hunts, secret trials, bannings, and such allied techniques?" Again, "At the same time we are acutely aware and we should be realistic enough to recognize that inevitably increasingly authoritarian methods will have to be implemented in a desperate attempt to maintain a system of structural injustice and oppression—which in turn will increase the number of persons affected."

These are extracted from his 1973 writings. By February, 1974, he could say, "This proposed legislation ['affected organization' proposals] now removes all doubt that South Africa is a police state." On September 20, 1976, the CI published its book entitled, *South Africa—A "Police State"?*, and Naudé in the Introduction wrote:

> The State can withdraw and deny passports without giving reasons; can deny information to the public; can close down newspapers; can decide where people must live, and for Africans, where they can work; can take people before courts on criminal charges which they, the Nationalists, have created and which would not be viewed as criminal in any civilized country of the world. The facts presented in this report tend to justify rather than mitigate the serious question of whether South Africa is now perhaps an "incomplete" Police State, if in fact not a Police State in the full sense of the word.
>
> We undertake this publication to convey our conviction to South Africa that a system of preventative detention for an indefinite period or detention without trial can never resolve the current crisis—the root cause whereof has to be sought in our inhuman and unjust racial policies.

Moreover, Naudé now felt that the obstinancy of most whites had reached the point where "I retain serious doubts of whether the developments toward a shared society would take place without serious confrontation which could include some form of violence."

To compound the gloom, Naudé's associate, the newly appointed director of the CI in Natal, Dr. Manas Buthelezi, the first Ph. D. in theology among the Africans (incidentally earned in the United States), was banned for five years in December, 1973. (For unknown reasons this ban was abruptly lifted in May, 1974. A major factor in the lifting could have been Dr. Buthelezi's suing Dr. John Poorter, editor of *To the Point,* for character assassination, since he had dared list unsubstantiated charges against him. He was awarded damages in October, 1975. Yet he was detained for a few days following the Soweto riots, and this was soon after he had become head of the Lutheran Church in South Africa.)

The Buthelezi affair is crucial because Naudé, besides daringly taunting the government to its face, was more and more aligning himself with the black cause, taking his stand with his friends among the African leaders. He was now a traitor not only to Afrikanerdom but also to all whites. "Kaffir-boetie" (nigger-lover) was the ultimate term of white contempt. In this step he was moving far beyond the liberalism of such dissidents as Alan Paton, who in the 1976 crisis had disclosed his own true colors: "One last word. There may be a war. Most of us will do what is expected of us. . . . We don't like being governed by the nats (National Party), but we'd rather be governed by them than by a Russian-Cuban sponsored government. Of course that's because we're white. If we were black we might think differently."

It was just this retreat into white racism of the more comprehensive and subtle form which Naudé had sought to avoid. Furthermore, it cannot be imagined that he would have endorsed fighting in its defense. Thus Naudé was being forced by circumstances beyond his control into a radicalism which he had not anticipated at the beginning, a radicalism which would be hard pressed to maintain a Christian hearing.

The stages toward this radicalism were ever so slight but nonetheless discernible. First was the Hammanskraal action in which Naudé took the lead in getting the South African Council of Churches to take a stand against the country's increasing dependence upon militarism. Second was Naudé's acceptance of the black consciousness movement, especially its formulations of black theology and its growing disenchantment with the traditional white assurances of a greater share of the capitalistic economy. And, finally, there was Naudé's inner feeling that the moment of truth had arrived for South Africa.

Where most whites were increasingly apprehensive of and bemoaning the signs of change, Naudé was seeing in these same events the hand of God's liberation. While he may not have been as exuberant as the aspiring Blacks who felt that any change, even that embracing riots, chaos, and anarchy, would be preferable to the status quo, Naudé was encouraged. This undisguised attitude on his part, plus his open endorsement of black identity and black power movements, further alienated him from the majority of whites. In this strange land of white and black neighbors of hundreds of years, there were not many friends of long standing and of genuine trustworthiness across racial lines, but it can be said that Naudé was one white who had now established nearly two decades of trying.

His annual Director's Report of October, 1976, heralded this new stage: "Of primary importance is the necessity of recognizing that the process of liberation is already under way, and that true liberation has to be welcomed by all of us. . . ." Just a few months earlier, in his address to the London audience, he had predicted: "The next two to three years would be the crucial period of decision-making in this regard, as I believe that white South Africa has only 5 to 6 years to put its house in order."

What separated him so dramatically from many of his liberal white friends, and what infuriated his opponents even more, was his express willingness to live under black rule. In the same London speech, he declared, "It is my clear conviction that, despite all efforts that the Government might currently or in the near future undertake to establish independent states, black majority rule for South Africa is inevitable. . . ." Therefore the business of the movement for the whites—since Naudé addresses himself unavoidably to the whites—is to prepare now for the transition. This resignation, as if it were a *fait accompli*, naturally cut against the grain of the die-hard preservers of white supremacy.

Adding fuel to the flames was the very wording of his calls for the whites to "shape up." In his September, 1976, Director's Report he called for Christian "support [for] all Black initiatives, especially those undertaken by clergy and lay Christian groups, to stimulate or promote the goal of liberation . . . which strengthens the growth of Black consciousness as a positive force for peaceful change." Here the word *all* would be inflammatory to most whites. Naudé and the CI encouraged such movements as the S.A. Student Organization, the Black Peoples Convention, the Black Community Programs, the Black Renaissance Conference, the African National Congress and the Pan

African Congress. Where Naudé looked with favor on these organizations, the government and most whites viewed them as subversive and headed by hired agitators.

On the question of the inevitable tie between racism and economic power, Naudé asked that "we as whites take seriously the black leaders' growing sense of the failure of capitalism to solve the problems of their oppression." Here the very mention of the phrase, "failure of capitalism," would trigger an emotional response.

What seemed premature and unwarranted to his critics was the way Naudé seemed to align himself totally with black disenchantment. Listening to Naudé, it was hard to tell where he left off reporting their attitudes and commenced giving his own opinion on the necessity of economic change. For instance, in his University of Natal speech, 1975, he reports: "What has become to them of crucial importance today is not only their insistence to share more meaningfully in the vast economic riches of the country, but something even much deeper: their strong belief that a fundamental change in the present economic system is essential to the achievement of true liberation of the black community." A year later in his Rhodes University speech he has adopted this position as his own: "There seems to me to be a lack of realisation within the commercial and industrial world of our country that our racial situation in SA is so serious that it requires a much fuller and more militant involvement of the economic sector. . . ."

In March of 1976 he and Chief Buthelezi issued a joint statement on "Foreign Investment in South Africa," calling for "a radical redistribution of wealth" and expressing the conviction that "capitalistic paternalism" had failed. The key sentence, however, was that "foreign investment in the central economy is devoid of all morality." Together they called "for a National Convention in which the Blacks of South Africa can speak for themselves on the matter of foreign investment." (For some time Naudé had been chairman of a study committee, along with Chief Buthelezi and two other scholars, investigating the influence of multi-national corporations in S.A., and a book reporting that study had been released, *Management Responsibility and African Employment in South Africa*.)

In taking on unqualifiedly, except on the method of non-violence, the cause of black liberation and linking this with his challenge of capitalism, had Naudé shouldered too much of the world, Atlas-like trying to support a whole new order? Some of his friends were beginning to feel that he had, along with his long-time enemies. Stephen Mulholland, writing in the *Business Times* of May 30, 1976, launched a scathing attack by saying, "Dr. Beyers Naudé presumably knows quite a lot about theology. He is, on the other hand, pitifully ignorant of the basics of economics." Over the years he had invited enough opposition as a "political parson"; now this little David had dared take on the Goliath of economics.

What must have been interpreted as the cruelest affront to classical economists was Naudé's seeing something good and creative in traditional African tribalism. Naudé saw the possibility of a "middle way" between capitalism and primitive communism, and called for serious studies to that effect. In his London speech he said, "but even if this is not allowed [by the S.A. authorities] the white minority group of South Africa should realize that if the African community in South Africa were free to express its aspirations, a form of African socialism equal to historic forms of African communalism which have always been operating within African societies, will be accepted, implemented and supported."

One concrete action on the part of the privileged sector of the capitalist economy which Naudé recommended was certainly not very radical, nor the least Marxist, but fully in line with the teachings of Jesus. This action suggested by Naudé was to assume a simpler life-style and to share with the less fortunate. Naudé writes, "One specific way in which the white community could prepare itself for the future is through the adoption of a new simplified life-style with a voluntary sharing of wealth and privilege. . . ." Speaking for himself and his associates, he referred to their willingness "to forego any increase in salary, despite the serious rise in cost of living, as a proof of their

sincerity in being willing to adapt themselves to a simpler life-
style and thus to lessen the seriously unjust gap in income between white and black wages which exists in our country."

What may not seem so radical in the larger world was within
the South African milieu of the moment considered almost
rabid. South Africa was harassed from without and from within.
Yet Naudé did not back away from his new positions: "Radical
change is a biblical concept—one which was fundamental to the
Christian Gospel long before any formulation of Marxist or Neo-
Marxist doctrines." In the Schlebusch Report he was accused of
trying to "embarrass the Government." Naudé, in reply, criti-
cized the Commission's failure to distinguish between the quest
for radical social change and Communist revolution. "Long before Marx our Lord Jesus promoted a cause of such and radical
change that it revolutionized the whole world," he retorted,
quoting Christ's words, "Behold, I make all things new!"

As we have said, Naudé's progression toward this radical
stance began with the SACC's Hammanskraal resolution of August 2, 1974. Its unique addition to his previous assessments and
recommendations rested in its proviso that "Christ's call to take
up the cross and follow Him in identifying with the oppressed
[means] in our situation becoming conscientious objectors.
. . . The Conference does not accept that it is automatically the
duty of those who follow Christ, the Prince of Peace, to engage
in violence and war, whenever the State demands it . . . [and]
points out that the Republic of South Africa is at present a
fundamentally unjust and discriminatory society." For the
South African citizen at large this was interpreted as a refusal
to fight for the country, in plain language, traitorous.

Even such a close friend of Naudé as Dr. Fred van Wyk, long
his top associate in the CI and currently head of the Institute
of Race Relations, took issue with it. In trying to respond to this
emotional wave of super-patriotism on the part of friends and
churches he had long counted on—for the action had split the
member churches down the middle—Naudé produced a call
for calmness and reconsideration. On this occasion, for the first
time, he takes the position that the struggle in Southern Africa

is a *civil war*. He begged his compatriots not to retreat to the monolithic stance of defending the status quo at any cost, but to seek a "third way": "that of evangelical rejection of violence, as a method of solving our problems. . . . This is the Christian way of reconciliation based on justice and freedom."

The government's response was to start proceedings at once to make it criminal to counsel any citizen in accordance with the Hammanskraal resolution. In turn this elicited from Naudé and the Christian Institute an even stronger call for defiance than their February statement. "We cannot and dare not surrender our duty to be pastors to the flock of Christ—and this includes the task of encouraging young people to face moral issues." The statement proceeds to say that such a law would plunge more and more young people into crises of conscience and make it impossible for any of them to decide between the demands of God for justice and the demands of their fatherland for unconditional loyalty. Instead it begs "the Government to take the positive step of providing conscientious objectors with the opportunity of performing non-military service while others are training for—or fighting—the war." This was proclaimed in October, 1974. In the meantime, Naudé's passport had been seized, his press was under indictment for allegedly publishing banned materials, and his appeals case was pending.

Yet in that year he was recipient of an honorary doctorate degree from the University of Witswatersrand in March and invited to Holland and to the United States, the latter in order to be the co-recipient of the Reinhold Niebuhr Award presented by the University of Chicago. The government, still playing a harrowing cat-and-mouse game with Naudé, in a surprise move returned his passport in time for him to make that trip in late November. No reasons were given, but perhaps the government was trying to appease two forces: the United Nations, with which it was in jeopardy at the moment, and the black African countries to the north, with which it was forming a new detente. (Just as precipitiously, his passport was seized again when he returned home from America.)

Nothing he said in his acceptance speech at the Niebuhr

Award ceremonies could have aroused the wrath of his country's officials, since his statement was mild and the opinions expressed had all been voiced before. He did, however, engage in a television debate while in Holland, and though the full text of that appearance is not available, perhaps official ire was provoked by his words to the effect that the South African government's momentary and apparent reversal of policy on apartheid and relations to Black Africa would necessitate a complete re-education in regard to everything it had pushed for the past twenty-five years. In his Chicago acceptance speech he reemphasized his adherence to liberation theology, his support of non-violence, his commitment to specific social change and the necessity of Christian sacrifice.

The mounting seas of troubles seem not to have restrained Naudé in his prophetic ventures in the least. Instead of resigning himself to despair in the face of the fulfillment of his realistic predictions, he looked upon these new crises as signs of hope and of God's intervention into human limitations. He writes in his Director's Report of 1975, "Taken all in all one can only conclude that this unjustified action against the Christian Institute ["affected organization status"] has been a blessing in disguise. . . ." Ironically, in the staff reductions made mandatory by the government's blow, the CI Board saw fit to release Naudé from the daily grind of the office in order for him to enlarge "his prophetic role."

But of course that had been his role all the time, because it was well known among his cohorts that, while he produced prodigiously and worked exceedingly well with his staff, he was ill-suited as an office manager or program technician. His personal buoyance under pressure, his radiant spirituality and his courageous devotion to following Christ, all made him a charismatic leader.

At the same time, this intensity of purpose, this single-mindedness in pressing for the Christian conversion of culture, could be misinterpreted as prophetic madness, the paranoid delusions of an excessively egotistic and introverted personality. This is exactly how many of his countrymen, and some of his friends, viewed him, and interpreted his oftentimes single-handed blows to straighten them out. They saw him taking upon himself the smug cloak of self-righteousness in assuming that his way was the only way. The judge in his trial had spoken of this inclination: "Perhaps you are in danger of making martyrs of yourself and members of your organization." Naudé's repeated claim, the identity between Christ's purposes and his own, naturally lent credibility to the charge of messianic pretensions.

He had wrestled with this problem of dogmatic conscience from the very moment of his awakening. In his famous Aasvoelkop sermon, he ponders aloud his anxiety:

> But how does one know when it is God who speaks? Does conscience tell us? And how do we know whether our conscience is always right? How did Peter know? How could he prove it? The fact was: he could not—he stood defenceless before his judges and before the people. The only anchor he had was the inner certainty of faith which God had given him through his Spirit—the certainty God gives to everyone who through conflict is prepared to come to total dependence on him and to be persuaded by him to that obedience which he expects of us. . . .

The other question is, how or why should it apply to South Africa?

> Now the question arises: what has all this to do with us? I know some will say: Is it not sheer audacity to draw an analogy from this story to the situation in which we find ourselves today. . . . Now I realise that there are many today who say: This is not the time to speak—even if many things are not right, or not morally defensible; this is the time to keep silent and to stand by your people. . . . What does it mean to follow God if it does not mean proclaiming the kingship of Jesus Christ over all peoples? . . . And when we as a Church fear or refuse to do this freely, then we let our people down—we betray our people.

Ten years later, in the heat of the pressure being placed upon himself and the Christian Institute, he envisioned, like Luther and Kierkegaard before him, a strong man whom God might raise up to straighten out the times:

> At this moment in our history our country urgently needs a person of stature, integrity, charismatic leadership and political acumen who has won the trust of both black and white to such a degree that both groups would be willing to entrust their future to his hands.

Did he not suspect deep within his soul that God had hammered himself out on the anvil of self-reflection, suffering and steadfastness under fire? "Our 'affected' life has thus become infused with a new clarity of insight, a hopefully deeper Christian commitment to the cause of liberation and a growing experience of facing joyfully greater sacrifice of ourselves for the sake of Christ and His Kingdom," he was able to write in the closing days of 1976.

By now "liberation" has become the passion of his life. Yet in examining his writings, one will look in vain for a liberation theology, developed and articulated. He has produced no full-length book, given no learned lectures outlining his thought. His is a piecemeal theology, done on-the-run (literally in the hide-and-seek escapades with his opposition), fired within the tensions of his daily witness. He simply has not had time to catch his breath, to retire to his study. He has been obliged to be on the front line mustering his troops, waving his flag. He would be the first to confess that he is not the person to formulate formal theology. Modestly, nonetheless accurately, he would claim that he is not prepared for that task.

Still, as one follows his career and peruses carefully his articles, his addresses, his critical broadsides on a burning issue, one can discern a well-developed thread of meaning. This thread of meaning will help explain Naudé's strength of character, his durability, his dialogic persuasiveness. If one of the tests of a prophet is whether he remains faithful to the very end—without copping out in favor of easy compromises and self-interest —another test is the verifiability of his word. On these two counts Naudé stands in the prophetic succession.

His version of liberation theology is best discovered in the study of his life—in his timely stands, in his arguments with his opposition, in both his long-term goals for his country and his passing accommodations, in his dialogue with the moderates within the camp and with the newly jelling parties among his cohorts, for example, those inclined toward black theology or Neo-Marxism. Therefore his version of liberation theology is different from the published varieties; it is not because he consciously tries to originate a new theology. It cannot be said that he is unaware of the main expressions of liberation theology in other lands—in Latin America, the Orient, Europe or the U.S.A. Both his journal and the Institute have kept these versions before the South Africa public. Rather, his liberation theology is born from his unique situation, and from his own rare response to that situation.

If a distinguishing mark of the catchall rubric, liberation theology, is the incarnation of the life of obedience to the God who moves ahead in history, then Naudé fully qualifies. Since his *metanoia* of the early 1960's, liberation theology has been lucidly reflected in his life. Freed from the confines of an unduly restrictive culture and church, from the confines of stultified dogmas involving racism, sexism, militarism, capitalism, statism, and even westernization, and from the confines of religion restricted to private piety, Naudé has been a freed personality, and has devoted himself fully and tirelessly to freeing others. In him we see liberation theology enacted in one man's career.

Whereas his declared enemies have tried to undermine him in public and arouse within him self-doubt, there is on the other hand a growing appreciation among the more mature and reflective citizenry of South Africa for his proven prophetic role. Using his own test articulated in the Aasvoelkop sermon—"the certainty God gives to everyone who through conflict is prepared to come to total dependence on Him"—Naudé has earned the title. For years he has searched his own conscience and has pressed the nation to search its conscience. When the prestigious University of Witswatersrand conferred upon him the honorary degree of Doctor of Laws in 1974, it cited this witness, and in particular a sermon Naudé delivered on the twenty-fifth anniversary of Human Rights Day, quoting it as follows:

Christians should prepare themselves spiritually and emotionally for the coming crisis. It is our duty to offer ourselves to stand on the side of Christ and of justice—regardless of whether this be on the side on which the Whites or the Blacks may be—and to give ourselves and all that we have in the peaceful struggle for truth, justice and love, regardless of whether we will be expedient, but whether we be right; not whether we succeed in the eyes of man, but whether we are obedient in the eyes of God; not whether we "ensure" our racial identity and security, but whether we prepare for the victory of the kingdom of God in our land.

POSTSCRIPT
A Personal Appreciation

Alan Paton and I sat one afternoon in 1959 at his home outside Durban where we were having tea. On that particular Sunday, Professor Arthur Keppel-Jones, the historian who had just prophesied South Africa's dismal future in his book, *When Smuts Goes,* had chosen to defect to Canada, and being on the high seas that very day the Sunday newspaper ran his full-page article entitled, "Why I'm Leaving South Africa." I asked Alan if Jones were a prophet. He parried by asking for a definition of a prophet. Hard pressed, I could think only of the Old Testament criterion: a prophet stays by God's people to suffer the very doom he predicts. Paton felt I had answered my own question. Later, during the years of our correspondence, Paton cited the rise of Beyers Naudé as God's true man. One letter soon after he had seen the first two copies of Naudé's new journal, *Pro Veritate,* in 1962, augured, "He certainly promises well, I think."

About the same time I managed to slip through the government's house-arrest barriers to interview the Zulu Chief, Albert Luthuli, a teacher in Christian schools later to receive the Nobel Peace Prize as the first Black South African and to write the telling autobiography, *Let My People Go.* When he learned I was from the southern United States and had worked with Martin Luther King in Georgia, he asserted abruptly, "I want to be the King of South Africa"—with a twinkle at the way his words had assembled. I countered, "Oh, but you already are!" "No-o-o, not me; not in this condition, confined to my compound, not able to meet, not able to communicate, not able to organize my followers." The government was clamping down on all expressions of African nationalism, and the party leaders, even the moderate, non-violent Luthuli, had all been silenced either by imprisonment or house arrest. He spoke with such painful impotence. The powerful had taken all the power away from such men as Alan Paton and Chief Luthuli. Or so they thought. But Paton and Luthuli had their own secret sources of power. And, paradoxically, born precisely within the stronghold of Afrikaner power itself, Naudé was being prepared to break forth. Like them, Naudé the powerless man was making his beginning moves against those in power.

Against the backdrop of celebrated names like Paton and Luthuli within the South African crucible would I interpret C.F.B. Naudé to an American audience. Or, for those readers more acquainted with the bravery of the German Christians who stood virtually alone against Hitler and the Nazi genocidal mania, Naudé may be compared to Dietrich Bonhoeffer, Karl Barth, and Martin Niemuller in sounding the Barmen warning and beginning the Confessional Church. Naudé's early conscientious dissent, his pioneering the church-state confrontation over his country's apartheid policy, over its violation of civil liberties, and over the increasing violence of its trend toward a police state—all at the greatest personal risk to himself—mark him as one of the heroes of the Christian resistance movement.

But I can speak more personally. As one who has lived in South Africa *before* and *after* Naudé, I can testify to the difference he has made in its climate of human relations, its theological realism, and the new responsibility on the part of its churches. *If* South Africa makes it through its present crisis, the transition to a truly multi-racial democracy, it can be said that Naudé *made the difference.* What Martin Luther King was to America, Naudé is to South Africa.

As a person who has worked throughout Africa (in over forty countries on assignments for Operation Crossroads Africa, African Theological Fund, Danforth Foundation, etc.), and having had residence in Nigeria, Kenya, Zambia, and South Africa, I would speak of Naudé's unique contribution to the black-white confrontation—one of God's laboratories for the coming together of the world's peoples.

As a person who admires him personally and knows him as a candidate for the Nobel Peace Prize, I would tell of his absolute devotedness to non-violence, of his irrepressible opposition to apartheid, of his higher patriotism in loving his country, of his obliviousness to personal risk in the face of the greedy octopus we all know as the military-industrial-national complex, and of his eagerness as a white to open his hand to, take his stand beside, and indeed live under black culture.

As a person who has been active in peace and liberation movements, I would liken him to Bishop Helda Camara in Latin America, to Daniel Dulci in Sicily, to Daniel Berrigan in the United States, and to those I dare not name in lands under Communism.

As a person who has lain awake at night in agony (spiritual battle and prayer) for those I love in the great fellowship of the saints, I would tell of that night in the spring of 1964 when all three—Martin Luther King, Clarence Jordan, and Naudé—were in my home together. If at that time I had predicted which one might be "bumped off" first I would have had to name Naudé. Yet the other two have been tragically removed and Naudé, now over sixty, has been spared to carry on even more daringly.

As one who was present at the organizational meeting of the Christian Institute in Johannesburg, who has contributed articles to *Pro Veritate,* who has accompanied Naudé on his rounds, and who has been a member of a CI Bible study group in Stellenbosch, I can attest to the sharpness of his analysis and to the contagion of his vision and hope.

As a person with healthy skepticism about the bourgeois person and his ability to alter his comfort-thing world, I would cite Naudé as a notable exception, a modern Saul of Tarsus whose radical decision in the early '60s at the mature age of forty-five, when his family had finally received its rewards from a series of successful parishes, turned him into a contemporary prophet, identified with *all* God's peoples.

A word of caution is in order. Within this record of Naudé's witness we have heard the church indicted as impotent, South Africa as a police state, and whites as obstinate and heartless. What the reader should never forget is that Naudé himself is also the church, a part of its best witness, one of its finest products. Naudé is also a South African and a white. He along with a minority of other South Africans who happen to be white but who have risen above the ethnocentrism of their compatriots are also an authentic product of their nationhood and history. I am not contradicting Naudé's words where he gives these indictments, for he of all persons should know. Rather I am saying that Naudé's appraisal issues from a lover's quarrel, and for him to take seriously his lover's quarrel implies the reality of a positive side, some response his own witness can count on. Naudé really believes they have the capacity for change, and, its counterpart, that God can affect change within South Africa.

South Africa is an old country, discovered before America and settled about the same time by white immigrants. Its history parallels America's: a British colony, slavery, a black-white confrontation, a democratic tradition. Much of Naudé's maneuverability as a prophetic witness has depended upon this tradition.

The country itself is a delightful landscape, again like America in its diversity and richness, and it has developed technologically not only as the top in Africa but in some ways advanced beyound western technocracies. Again, its people are warm, outgoing, energetic and resilient, rich in culture, both its white immigrant population (also Indian and Malay) and its majority of African originals.

Above all is the rich and diverse religious heritage, a mixture of the world's religions. Christianity's greatest missionary impact may be in South Africa, beginning with the Portugese and then the Moravians who pioneered missionary endeavor in the early 1700's and reaching its peak in British missionaries like Moffat and Livingstone. To this day few western nations have maintained such interest in church-going and in the church as community center. (Billy Graham made his first appearance in South Africa in 1974 to a mass rally before an integrated stadium in Durban.) Well known is the stalwart Calvinistic heritage in the Afrikaner culture. This factor in itself is enough to explain the mixed reception which Naudé receives: the self-interested ruling powers want to respect their best religious feelings but dare not let it interfere with their own goals; the churches are content with a culture-affirming piety yet nonetheless stand guilt-striken by the challenge of Christ to remake the whole culture. Therefore Naudé's enemies approach from two directions: he is a prophet without honor in his country's best political and religious traditions.

With such resources, though, how could a country fail? How could it be so tragic? It is best viewed as a healthy mixture, as a kaleidoscopic land. Its potential is great. The whole world has a stake in how South Africa goes. In the truest sense it can be called God's laboratory, where the testing for the world's future society is underway. Within its crucible Naudé is the catalyst.

I do not wish to leave the impression that Naudé is superhuman. Quite the contrary, he impresses all-comers as quite an ordinary man, deceptively so—in his dress, in his mannerisms, in his speech, in his total character cut from the authentic Afrikaner mold. This redounds to his very strength. One is disarmed by this first impression. Neither is he overbearing or threatening in an aggressive political profile. He is not even a profound writer, platform orator, or theological theorist. What *charisma* he has is altogether given, as it should be, not the part of a play-actor. What does come across powerfully is his sincerity and dedication. He appeals to the moral reservoir latent in every human breast. Law Professor Antony Allott of the International Commission of Jurists, sent to observe Naudé's trial, spoke of the feeling pervading the crowded Pretoria courtroom "as akin to the joyful spirit of the Early Christians before a public interrogation. Over the four days one asked himself repeatedly: 'Just who is standing trial in this courtroom?' "

If the final test of a prophet is perseverance, to stick by one's people through the very doom one has spent his life energies trying to get them to avoid, then Naudé qualifies. Naudé will die in behalf of the regeneration of his country. At this stage of his life it appears immaterial as to how and when death comes. He has risen above such concerns; his destiny is in God's hands. And that same destiny is what he wants most of all for South Africa.

APPENDIX

Events in the Life
of Beyers Naudé

Documents Crucial
to the Crises

APPENDIX CONTENTS

Events in the Life of Beyers Naudé

Born May 10, 1915

1932–39 B.A., M.A., and theological degree, Stellenbosch University

1939–54 Pastorates at Wellington, Laxton, Pretoria-South

1955–59 Potchefstroom pastorate

1957 Reformed Ecumenical Synod, Potchefstroom

1958–62 Acting Moderator of Transvaal Synod

1963 Elected Moderator of Transvaal Synod

1959–63 Organizer and pastor of Aasvoelkop Church in suburbs of Johannesburg

1960 March, Sharpeville riots and the police shootings
December, Cottesloe Consultation, between South African Churches and World Council of Churches

1961 April, Transvaal Synod renounces the Cottesloe Resolutions and votes to withdraw from WCC

1962 May 15, first issue of *Pro Veritate*, Naudé editor

1963 March, resignation from the Broederbond
August, founding of the Christian Institute
September, denied clergy status by Dutch Reformed Church
September, resignation sermon from Aasvoelkop Church, "Obey God, Rather than Man"

1964 Harassment by the Secret Police

1965 Naudé and Geyser libel suit against Professor Pont

1966 October, NGK Synod condemns Christian Institute

1969 Ulvenhout Consultation, Holland

1972   October 20, honorary doctorate, Free University of Amsterdam

1973   February 27, decision to defy the Schlebusch Commission

September 24, arrest

November 13, trial commences

December 2, Naudé's appeal reversed; remains under conviction

1974   Spring, honorary doctorate, University of Witswatersrand

August 2, Hammanskraal Statement of South African Council of Churches

November, recipient of the Niebuhr Award, University of Chicago

1975   May, "Responsible Liberation," speech read in absentia to J'Accuse Club, Holland

May and June, release of Schlebusch Report and the Christian Institute and *Pro Veritate* declared "affected organizations"

August 22, "A Glimpse into the Future of South Africa," a speech to the University of Natal

September 15, Horst Kleinschmidt, Naudé's assistant, detained

December 16, "The Individual and the State in South Africa," speech read in absentia before the Royal Institute of International Affairs, London

1976   March 10, "Foreign Investment in South Africa," joint statement by Chief Buthelezi and Naudé

April 30, *Detention and Detente in Southern Africa,* book published by the Christian Institute with Introduction by Naudé

June 3, "The South Africa I Want," speech to University of Capetown

August, Naudé's statement on Soweto; detention of Jane Phakathi, Naudé's Transvaal Director

September 18, Christian Institute's Resolutions

September 20, *South Africa: A "Police State"?* book published by the Christian Institute with Introduction by Naudé; immediately banned

September 28, "Foreign Investment in South Africa," speech to Rhodes University

October 31, "Message to Christians in Europe"

November 25, Raid on the CI offices in Capetown and the arrest of Cedric Mayson, editor of *Pro Veritate*

1977   February 4, "The Afrikaner as Rebel," University of Capetown lecture

February issue of *Pro Veritate* banned

March 16, Jane Phakathi, Naudé's Transvaal assistant, issued a banning order for five years

April 4, Naudé's Easter Message

September, Steve Biko's mysterious prison death and Jane Phakati flees to Holland

October 19, Naudé banned for five years

My Decision
OBEDIENCE TO GOD
(Acts 5:17–42)

Acts 5:29 We must obey God rather than men.

Our text this morning is taken from Acts 5:29 which reads "We must obey God rather than men."

To understand what these words mean for the Church and for society, and also for you and me, we must begin by clearly understanding their context.

Here we see a group of men and women (actively) proclaiming Jesus Christ as he revealed himself to them by the outpouring of the Holy Spirit. Their proclamation is not just a recitation of history; it is certainly history, resurrection history, but it is much more: it is a witness to Jesus Christ, as Resurrected Lord, as the Living One in their midst. And because he is alive, they experience his life in them, they experience a transformation and renewal of their whole being. Their message is of Easter and Pentecost, of the gift of new, divine life affecting every aspect of human life and transforming all human relationships. Is it any wonder that this message brought many to total acceptance, but just as many others to fierce resistance?

Now the word of Scripture becomes a vivid truth of experience for the apostles: the Gospel is a sign which shall be spoken against, a savour of life unto life and death unto death, a word active and powerful and sharper than any two-edged sword. That this sword cuts two ways is clear as the opposition reveals itself—and this from the side of the high priest and the Sadducean party which called together the Sanhedrin as an ecclesiastical body, before which Peter and the apostles must present themselves—the same body, this, which condemned Jesus. The high priest is perturbed that the apostles have ignored the previous command no longer to teach in the Name of Jesus Christ: the Sanhedrin had hoped by persuasion to impose silence on the apostles. Now they accuse the apostles of disturb-

ing the peace of Jerusalem ("You have filled Jerusalem with
your teaching") and the peace of the church with a message
which they classify as self-willed ("your teaching") and they
reprove the apostles for trying to lay the death of this Man at
their door. Had they so soon forgotten that but a short while
before precisely this was the wish expressed by the people
before Pilate: "Let his blood be upon us and upon our children!"

What defence can Peter and the apostles offer? Apparently
the charge is well grounded. They have been disobedient. What
can Peter say by way of rebuttal? How peculiar: he offers no
defence whatsoever. He could, had he wished, have referred to
the recent miraculous works of healing and the equally miraculous release from the prison the previous night, but he does not
even mention it. What he does do is this: he brings them face
to face with God as they have come to know him in and through
Jesus Christ. Peter says, briefly and boldly: when God com-
mands, all else must give way. This does not mean that human
authorities and powers must not be obeyed. On the contrary:
"Let every man be subject to the powers set over him" says
Paul. However, when the will of man conflicts with the will of
God, then man must realise: now I must obey God rather than
man.

But how does one know when it is God who speaks? Does
conscience tell us? And how do we know whether our conscience is always right? How did Peter know? How could he
prove it? The fact was: he could not—he stood defenceless before his judges and before the people. The only anchor he had
was the inner certainty of faith which God had given him
through his Spirit—the certainty God gives to everyone who
through conflict is prepared to come to total dependence on
him and to be persuaded by him to that obedience which he
expects of us.

In this shining certainty, the apostles now offer to their
church and people in the name of the living Christ, salvation
and forgiveness of sin. Their message to the Sanhedrin is: Christ
is ready to make a new beginning with the ancient people of
Israel; the door is still open; his grace is available (vv. 30–32)
And they? What do they make of this offer?

The reaction of the Sanhedrin is immediate and sharp (v. 33). The words pierce their hearts (but in quite the opposite way to that of the crowds of Pentecost) and arouse enmity and resistance, resentment and anger.

But amongst them is Gamaliël, the well-known Jewish theologian, highly respected by his people—the man to whom we usually refer as the sage counsellor of the Sanhedrin. In a way this is true: what Gamaliël says contains much wisdom and truth. But when we look more deeply, we realise that he is not concerned with Christ, the Truth and the Wisdom of God. His real concern is not for the apostles, i.e. for Jesus, but for the Sanhedrin, the Jews. He speaks a word of warning ("For if this idea of theirs or its execution is of human origin, it will collapse; but if it is from God, you will never be able to put them down, and you risk finding yourselves at war with God.") a word whose prophetic truth and import he does not appreciate—just as Caiaphas is unwittingly used by God to speak prophetically when he said of Jesus "it is more to your interest that one man should die for the people than that the whole nation should be destroyed."

What does Gamaliël's advice amount to? Do you know? "Postpone the decision: do nothing now—the time is not yet ripe." I believe Gamaliël perceived the integrity of the apostles; I believe he felt very unhappy about the course of events in the Sanhedrin—but in his counsel he avoids a decision, and leads his people away from Jesus by a devious path!

And the conclusion of the whole matter? The apostles rejoiced that they were counted worthy to suffer for their Master, and they continued with their teaching—**disobedient yet at the deepest level obedient, unfaithful, yet faithful at the deepest level.**

Thus far the exposition. Now the question arises: what has all this to do with us? With you, with me, with the situation in our church, in our people, in South Africa and in Africa? I know some will say: Is it not sheer audacity to draw an analogy from this story to the situation in which we find ourselves today? Only the Holy Spirit, my brethren, can persuade each one of you to what extent Acts 5 applies to our situation. As for myself

I have tried to find guidance for my own decision in other passages of Scripture, and I have tried to find reasons which would enable me to sever my connection with Pro Veritate and the Christian Institute and continue peacefully and happily with my pastoral work. But time and again—sometimes with great conflict, fear and resistance in my heart—the Lord brought me back to this passage of Scripture, as if to say: whatever this text may mean for others, this is my answer for you: obey God rather than man!

And now I pass on to you the insight as God has given it to me in recent days, through many events, and sometimes with great resistance and unwillingness on my part:

The decisions of Synods, Presbyteries and Sessions, and the consequent reactions, have clearly indicated to me that although the Synod has not in so many words prohibited pronouncements which are not in accordance with church policy and the traditions of the past, in spirit and in practice these decisions come to this: that the God-given right and freedom of minister and member to witness to the truth of God's Word in the spirit of the prophets and the reformers is so restricted that the minister of the Gospel in principle no longer enjoys the freedom to declare his deepest Christian convictions in the way or at the place and time given him by God to speak through his Word and Spirit.

Consequently the choice facing me is not primarily a choice between pastoral work and other Christian work or between the Church and Pro Veritate, or between the Church and the Institute. No, the choice goes much deeper: it is a choice between obedience in faith and subjection to the authority of the Church. And by unconditional obedience to the latter, I would save face but lose my soul.

By joining the Christian Institute, I am not leaving the Church. On the contrary, I wish, through the Institute, to serve my church in the wider ecumenical content, even if my church today does not officially see it in this light, or so desire it. Nor am I abandoning the ministry of the Word—for this very reason, I applied for permission to retain my status in order to show my church that I did not wish to be anything other than a minister of the Word. Concerning the decision of the Examining Commission I would only say that I regard it as unreasonable and unjustified—a decision which cannot be upheld on the basis of ecclesiastical policy nor founded on precedent. And so I pray that the day may soon dawn when this decision will be rescinded. In the meantime there is only one way for me: to be obedient to God! This is God's Word and Way for me. Therefore I must go.

But this text has a meaning for this congregation—because this step of mine affects you even though neither you nor I willed it so. You also are called upon to choose, to decide. You cannot escape it. And please note: the decision has nothing to do with my person or convictions, with my remaining with or leaving the congregation, or with your views about Pro Veritate or the Christian Institute—fundamentally it concerns Christ. The question is: do you see his word as your final authority? If so, obey his word. Do you live by his word? God will not let you go until you have chosen!

For our Dutch Reformed Church also, our text this morning has a meaning. We are in such a specially privileged, and therefore all the more responsible, position, that the voice of our Church ranges far and can exercise great influence. The life of our Dutch Reformed Church is interwoven with the life of our people in this time when our existence is threatened. And every true Afrikaner is deeply in sympathy with his people in this anxious time (and I associate myself with them as an Afrikaner who, just as in the past, today still wishes to serve his people with the same love and faithfulness.)

Now I realise that there are many today who say: This is not the time to speak—even if many things are not right, or not morally defensible: this is the time to keep silent and to stand by your people. Brethren, no matter how well-intentioned such a view may be, do we not as Christians understand that such an attitude is born of fear, and that fear is a sign of unbelief? Do we not believe that if we obey God in all things according to his Word, we can leave our future and that of our people with safety in his hands? Whose kingdom comes first: The Kingdom of God, or that of our people? Which is more important: that we stand together or that we all follow God? And what does it mean to follow God if it does not mean proclaiming the kingship of Jesus Christ over all peoples (and therefore also over our people)—and this applies also to our ecumenical and race relations? And when we as a Church fear or refuse to do this freely, then we let our people down—we betray our people!

If the D.R. Church will not take heed and carry out this obedience which God demands, then we shall suffer endless damage and sorrow. Not only will we lose or frustrate some of the best intellectual and spiritual powers in our ministerial ranks, not only will we lose the confidence of thousands of members who seek more Scriptural illumination on all these burning questions of Church and state, of kingdom and people, of race and colour without finding it in their Church—even more: our Church is irrevocably estranging the affections of our "daughter" churches and closing the door in the face of its witness to the churches of Africa. If our Church continues with this conscious and fear-inspired process of isolation with its tragic withdrawal from the Holy Catholic Church in South Africa and Africa, we shall, spiritually, wilt and die! O my Church, I call today with all the earnestness that is in me: awake before it is too late, stand up and stretch out the hand of Christian brotherhood to all who reach out to you in sincerity! There is still time, but time is becoming short, very short.

But also for us as ministers of the word, Acts 5:29 has meaning. Very many ministers are deeply concerned about the course of events in our Church. Many are concerned because it appears that the Church is not free to act solely on the authority of God's Word because other influences and powers are playing the dominant rôle. Many are convinced that great changes will have to take place in our ecclesiastical and race relations on many levels. But for various reasons they suppress these convictions:—the fear that if they speak, the Church will be harmed,—the fear that our members are not yet ready to accept these truths,—the possible repercussions in our congregations.

In such a situation we are all called to act with the utmost responsibility, but certainly not to remain silent. The proclamation of the truth of the Gospel cannot harm the Church of Jesus Christ! And if our members are not influenced by all sorts of other powers but are enlightened fully and fearlessly as to just what the Word of God requires of all people (white as well as non-white), then will the Spirit of God not lead them into all truth? Why then do we fear? Has the time not arrived for us to proclaim clearly and with joy: **Thus saith the Lord?**

Finally: this text has meaning also for the other churches in South Africa and for the Christians in those churches (white as well as non-white). You who with us confess faith in Christ and his Word: is your first obedience and your highest loyalty to Christ? Are you prepared to call on your people to seek this obedience and set it above all else? Even where it conflicts with their deepest human sentiments? Are you prepared to recognise injustice where injustice has occurred (also against the Afrikaner) to give love and sympathy where it is needed and to humble yourself so that Christ may be magnified?

To all Christians of all churches and peoples and languages and races who sincerely seek and pray for this highest obedience to God comes his glorious assurance even for the unsure future: If God is for us, who can be against us?

Amen.

Rev. C.F.B. Naudé
Sermon from "My Decision"
Published by the Christian Institute

Twelve Statements for the Consideration of All Christian Voters . . .

For a long time now, an awareness has been growing among a large number of Christians that something must be **done**, especially in the **political** field, to counter the deteriorating human relations in our country. The voting public of South Africa in general—which so often prides itself as being Christian—and specifically the responsibility that the Christian as citizen carries, need to be confronted by way of a clear Christian witness with the real demands of Christian responsibility. The following manifesto, which is being made public during the week-end of 17th-18th January, 1970 was drawn up with a view to the impending General Election. It is a first step in this direction.

Twelve Statements for the Consideration of All Christian Voters in the Republic of South Africa

1. Every Christian has an inescapable political responsibility, especially he who has the vote.

2. Politics concerns itself with the arrangement of society and therefore most intimately affects the lives of people created in the image of God.

3. It is the Christian's duty to contribute by his vote towards the establishment of a government which shall promote law and order, and shall work for the welfare of the whole community over which it is appointed, in accordance with the Biblical commandments of truth, justice and love.

4. Any arrangement of a people's life which is not in accordance with the commandments of truth, justice and love opposes the common good, endangers law and order, conflicts with the will of God and therefore leads to the downfall of such a people.

5. In His acts of creation and of salvation, God reveals that He is deeply concerned about human society as well as about the life and fate of every individual. This is why the Christian recognises the intrinsic value of society and the dignity of every individual.

6. The Christian shares in the responsibility for the arrangement of society in accordance with the revealed commandments and promises of God. Hence, in his political witness and action, he should be obedient to the revealed will of God and reject anything which conflicts with it.

7. Every Christian must, therefore, give account to God concerning his giving or withholding of support for any particular political party and its policy. He should test his own participation in politics by the following basic standards.

8. RECONCILIATION. In obedience to God, no Christian can support a political policy which is based on an unjust discrimination, on arbitrary grounds of colour, race, religion or sex, between people who live and work in the same country. He must further reject such a policy of discrimination when it leads to a consistent enforced separation of such people without their common consent. Man's sinful urge towards discrimination and separation stands in direct conflict with the Bible's message of reconciliation.

9. TRUTH. In obedience to God, no Christian can support a political policy which, being demonstrably impracticable, bases its appeal to the electorate on false claims and promises. Such an essentially dishonest policy cannot be reconciled with the Christian's commitment to the truth.

10. JUSTICE. In obedience to God, no Christian can support a political policy which, for its practical implementation, unavoidably necessitates open or concealed injustice towards any individual or population group. A policy which essentially diminishes, offends or injures the human dignity of any citizen must be totally rejected by the Christian.

11. LOVE. In obedience to God, no Christian can support a political policy which is essentially based on group selfishness and the furtherance of sectional interests only. Such a policy leads to inhumanity and lovelessness and must consequently clash with the law of love given by Christ.

12. It is the Christian's grave duty and responsibility thoroughly to examine the policy of every political party in South Africa and to acquaint himself with its implications. He must weigh all political utterances and policies against the truth of God. In so doing, he may find that no available political policy represents complete obedience to this truth; he will nevertheless be obliged, in making his judgment, to approach as closely as possible to a complete obedience.

The Christian who has the vote must guard against the temptation to make decisions based on personal or group selfishness. His responsibility becomes even greater in a society where a small minority of citizens elect the members of the central parliament.

In short, the Christian's participation in politics must be determined by his inescapable responsibility towards God and his neighbour.

(*Pro Veritate,* January 1970)

Weighed And . . . ?

DRAMATIC SEQUEL TO GOVERNMENT BAN ON NUSAS LEADERS
Christian Institute Shock Boycott Move
Refuse to testify before
Schlebusch Commission

Members of the Board of Management and executive staff of the Christian Institute—the next organisation to be investigated by the Schlebusch Commission—will refuse, at the risk of heavy fines or jail sentences, to give evidence before the Commission or to co-operate in its inquiry in any way.

Their stand is fully backed by the board of the institute. The board has passed a resolution affirming its support for those of the board and staff executive "who decide that in conscience they cannot co-operate with a Commission of Inquiry which they consider, by its constitution and mandate, to be a denial of the democratic process and judicial procedure."

A letter informing the Commission of the institute's decision was handed to the Deputy Secretary of the House of Assembly, Mr. P. J. G. Venter, by the regional director of the institute, the Rev. Theo Kotzé, in Cape Town on Friday.

Dr. Naudé said yesterday: "I wish to make it quite clear that this is not a political decision. It is rather a matter of deep moral conviction on the part of the staff and board members who have taken the decision, and I deeply respect such a stand."

The Letter

The letter handed to the Commission read:

"During the meetings of the Board of Management of the Christian Institute of Southern Africa, held over the weekend of March 2–4, the pending investigation of the Christian Institute by a Parliamentary Select Commission was discussed.

"A number of board and executive staff members stated that they could not in conscience participate in this investigation.

The Board of Management resolved as follows:

"1. That the recent action taken against student leaders by way of arbitrary banning orders confirms our initial impression that the thinking behind the appointment of the Parliamentary Select Committee is calculated to permit punitive measures being taken under the guise of democratic procedure.

"2. That we reaffirm our conviction that the investigation of any organisation should be undertaken through a judicial commission which can ensure impartiality, the right of defence to accusations made, the right to face one's accusers and the upholding of the due process of law.

"3. That we fully support those of the board and staff executive who decide that in conscience they cannot co-operate with a Commission of Inquiry, which they consider by its constitution and mandate to be a denial of the democratic process and judicial procedure.

"4. That while we confidently affirm that we have nothing to hide, we also affirm that there is much to preserve by way of our Christian heritage of fairness and the evidencing of justice, which such a Parliamentary Commission palpably erodes."

Mr. Brown said that if an impartial judicial commission had been set up to inquire into the activities and objectives of the Christian Institute, its members would not have hesitated in co-operating with it fully.

The Schlebusch Commission, appointed as a Parliamentary Select Committee and changed into a commission, is made up of ten Members of Parliament—six Nationalists and four from the United Party.

It was set up to inquire into the report on the activities of four anti-apartheid organisations—the National Union of South African Students (Nusas), the Institute of Race Relations, the Christian Institute and the University Christian Movement.

The first investigation was into Nusas, whose members gave evidence before the Commission when called on to do so. The Commission's interim report on Nusas, released last week, resulted in the Government banning eight student leaders.

—Sunday Times, 11.3.73
(*Pro Veritate*, March 1973)

Statement by Staff Members of the Christian Institute

Given to the *Sunday Times* 11th August, 1973

We who have appended our names to this statement wish to make known our resolve not to testify before the Schlebusch Commission, even if subpoenaed to do so.

As followers of Christ, we accept and wish to obey Him as our highest authority, and therefore we regard any co-operation in this matter to be a betrayal of our Lord. This stand is in accord with the recent manifesto for "Christian Change" published by the Institute, which states: "Law and Government are subject to the Gospel of Christ and injustice and totalitarian activities must be rejected. Faced by unchristian laws, Christians should obey God rather than man."

We wish to reiterate the call of the Christian Institute to the Government to respect the due process of law and not to disregard the judiciary in this matter. The Government having appointed a Commission which by its mandate undermines the democratic procedure and the rule of law, we are not prepared to acquiesce in this.

No citizen who has the cause of truth and justice at heart would willingly wish himself or his fellow citizens to be subjected to an enquiry in which:

A charge, if any, is undefined;

Accusers, if any, can never be faced and challenged;

Proceedings are in secret and every person testifying is sworn to secrecy, thus allowing shapeless charges by faceless men in the dark;

No right of defence or repudiation of untruth or falsehood is thus possible;

The Commission alone decides what shall be made public.

The Minister of Justice recently made it clear that the Government is prepared to bend or even break the rule of law when it sees fit. Have we come to this pass that we can no longer be governed save by abominations peculiar to Communistic and totalitarian lands such as state witch-hunts, secret trials, bannings and such allied techniques?

We are in conscience bound to oppose such and other totalitarian methods as a form of evil which is destroying the soul of our people, especially of the Whites.

The situation is made all the more serious because the Government is in this instance being aided and abetted by the official Opposition which is collaborating in this process through its participation in the Schlebusch Commission, thereby leaving the principles of justice and fairness that are part of the legal and moral fibre of our society to the mercy of politicians.

Believing our stand to be one of conscience and under Divine constraint we re-affirm:

(1) We have nothing to hide;
(2) We will co-operate fully with an open Judicial Enquiry;
(3) There is nothing of significance the Government does not already know about the Christian Institute;
(4) If the Government had a legitimate case against the Christian Institute or its staff they would institute court proceedings;
(5) Recent arbitrary bannings and punitive actions give us grounds to believe that such investigations are used as the pretext for some non-judicial action.

Freedom is indivisible. What is done to us today may well be done to others tomorrow. Let us be mindful that no man is an island unto himself. Therefore "send not to ask for whom the bell tolls—it tolls for thee."

We call upon all lovers of truth and righteousness to oppose all that which frustrates God's will within our nation. For righteousness and truth alone exalt a nation.

Signed:

Dr. C. F. Beyers Naudé—Director

The Rev. Theo Kotzé—Cape Regional Director

The Rev. Brian Brown—Administrative Director

Mrs. Jane Phakathi—Community Organiser

The Rev. Roelf Meyer—Editor of *Pro Veritate* and Study Secretary

Eloquent Silence or Co-operation?

The State propaganda machine is poised to make political capital out of the declared intention of certain Christian Institute staff members not to testify before the Schlebusch Commission, and inevitably the Christian Institute will be discredited as "having something to hide."

It will be our task constantly to spell out just why this non-participation by some has been decided upon, and in doing so the privilege of witness will be ours.

Significantly, in recent days a cabinet minister declared that the Government would act as it sees fit, irrespective of the rule of law. This admission confirms the C.I.'s contention that the Government has introduced a strain of lawlessness into public affairs, contributed to a progressive erosion of respect for law and order, and in this instance disregarded the authority of the judiciary.

The C.I. has, in vain, persistently asked the legislature to respect the due processes of law by appointing a Judicial Commission. Words having failed, those who seek to follow the biblical tradition of the prophet are perhaps obliged to embrace the discipline of symbolic action. Perhaps it is necessary that some of our staff risk imprisonment so that John Citizen might ask: "Has it come to this?"

For let us again declare what it has come to:

> Proceedings of the Schlebusch Commission are in secret;
> The commission determines what shall be divulged for public consumption and what shall not;
> The one testifying is sworn to secrecy, which can mean subsequent gagging despite awareness of misrepresentation;
> No knowledge of allegations made against one's person or organisation is necessarily conveyed, with no right of defence or repudiation in consequence;
> And while one does not attribute partiality as inevitable, one appreciates the frightful dilemma of parliamentarians investigating a body opposed to every iniquity of the very apartheid scheme which they propagate.

Is this fair? No member of the Commission could respond to this question affirmatively, and no self-respecting citizen would wish to be placed in such a vulnerable position.

Furthermore, recent arbitrary bannings and punitive actions have shown that the Government delights in an "investigation" as the pretext for some non-judicial action. Some of us are now called to repudiate this cloaking of darkness in the guise of light. For if the Government had any legitimate case against the Christian Institute (and they assuredly know all about us!) they would not waste a minute in instituting court proceedings.

At his trial one called Jesus stood before his accusers and "as a lamb to the slaughter," was dumb. Was his point weak, and did he have something to hide? Or has history interpreted that eloquent silence by reversing the roles of accuser and accused?

(Published by The Christian Institute of Southern Africa, August 1973)

Weighed and . . . ?

PRESS STATEMENT ON THE SCHLEBUSCH COMMISSION

We have no option but to refuse to testify before the Schlebusch Commission. In conscience, we have had no other option since eight of our fellow citizens were arbitrarily deprived of their basic human freedoms as a result of the secret investigation of this body of party politicians. The fact that one of these politicians has actually changed his allegiance and presumably his principles during the course of the investigation confirms our viewpoint that politicians are not suitably qualified to sit in impartial judgement on their political opponents. We recall the words of one commentator who said that the punitive action taken as a result of the Commission's investigation was based on evidence insufficient "to hang a cat."

It would be a naïve person indeed who did not believe that anyone appearing before the Commission is potentially on trial for his political views, without knowing his accusers or the charges or the evidence against him, and without the right to cross-examine those who testify against him. Above all, this "trial" is conducted in secret, so that justice cannot be seen to be done. We are prepared to testify before an independent judicial commission or to face any charges in open court. As believers in democracy and justice we refuse to participate in a process that prostitutes both democracy and justice.

Our refusal should be seen not so much as disobedience to the state, as obedience to the demands of a higher standard of morality and justice. We recall that our Lord Himself refused to answer questions at His own unfair and unjust interrogations. The ruling powers are servants of God which means that they cannot raise themselves arbitrarily above the norms of justice and fairness without violating the highest authority. If they do this the ruling powers become the evil ones who must be opposed in obedience to God.

We view with particular abhorrence the role of the official opposition in this prostitution of normal democratic processes. We reject utterly the reasons advanced by the leader of the opposition for his party's continued participation in the Schlebusch Commission. He and his party cannot be absolved from the shame of arbitrary action against people who must be presumed innocent since no charge against them has been proved. They cannot be absolved from responsibility for the action that will be taken against us for our refusal to testify. We have tried every reasonable means to persuade Sir de Villiers Graaff to withdraw his party from the Commission, but these efforts have met with bland refusal. We do not believe that the sole United Party representative on the sub-committee investigating us, Mr. Wm. Morris Sutton, can ensure "a fair and just hearing," which was the official reason given by his party for its participation on the Commission. We consequently call on him, following the precedent of his colleagues on the select committee on Bantustan consolidation, to lay down his "cross" and withdraw immediately.

We believe that Sir de Villiers Graaff and those in his party who have insisted on continued participation in the Commission are guilty, at best, of a grave error of judgement and that history will judge them in the harshest terms, since the collaboration of the United Party might be seen as lending some degree of credibility to this travesty of parliamentary democracy.

> *Signed:*
> Beyers Naudé   Horst Kleinschmidt
> Roelf Meyer   Peter Randall
> Danie van Zyl   Theo Kotzé
> Brian Brown   Dot Cleminshaw
>   September 1973
>   (*Pro Veritate,* October 1973)

The Christian Principles for Which the Christian Institute Stands in Southern Africa

1. THE BASIS

The revelation of God in Christ is the basis of the Christian's belief and behaviour. The Old Testament expresses God's purpose to liberate Israel in all her social, economic and political life. This purpose is fulfilled and extended in Christ to the whole of human society. Within that vast corporate concern God reaches out in tender care with the offer of individual salvation now and forever.

Our response to God must be spiritual and temporal, and must be expressed both corporately and individually.

* All the fundamental problems of the world are found to some degree in South Africa. Our task as Christians is to follow the Gospel through which God can renew the life and society of this sub-continent on which we live.

2. THE GOOD NEWS OF JESUS CHRIST

2.1 Jesus Christ is Lord

He is the Lord of human society, proclaiming the sovereignty of God and sending out His friends to call every part of the world to follow Him. He is the Lord of our whole life.

Responding to His authority Christians seek a developing society where all may find that love which leads to peace and prosperity, to justice and joy, to responsibility and freedom, and where they may live in harmony and godly love.

* In Southern Africa some people acknowledge the lordship of other gods: the supreme importance of race, apartheid, 'Christian nationalism,' denominationalism, and a self-centred piety.

2.2 Jesus Christ is Saviour

In their individual lives and in their institutions men suffer because of sin. They are alienated from God, and live in an alienated society.

The Gospel awakens men to the reality and peril of sin, brings the message of the life, the cross and resurrection of Christ as the saving act of God and leads them through repentance and faith to a new life of fellowship with God and their neighbours.

* Southern Africa is a sick society because of its alienation and doomed to die unless it is healed. In this situation we all share. Our only hope is to admit our need of Christ, to turn to Him in personal and national repentance, and to trust Him and follow His ways for salvation.

3. THE CHRISTIAN COMMUNITY

3.1 Opportunity

God made man as a creative and responsible being, and in Christ sets him free to develop his whole life and that of his fellowmen.

Christians seek social conditions where each person can develop his creative abilities to the maximum, and grow in stature by fulfilling the responsibilities of manhood.

* The social structure of South Africa prevents most people from developing their full potential because of their colour. Christian change means opening equal opportunities to all in the fields of education, economics, politics, law and the church.

3.2 Fellowship

God summons man to communion with his Creator and his fellowmen. People are isolated in a disrupted community because of sin; in Christ, God brings them into a restored community of love.

Christians should seek to establish conditions in which people may enjoy the fullness of human fellowship in the whole of society.

* In South Africa people of different racial backgrounds are kept apart. Whites are not permitted to visit blacks freely in their homes, and apartheid legislation has the inevitable result of breaking up family life. Christian change means the abolition of divisive legislation.

3.3 Sharing

The earth and its riches belong to God who has set people to live on it as His stewards in harmony, as epitomised by the spirit of the early Christians who shared their wealth.

Christians should seek a society in which land, wealth, and power can be equally obtainable by all.

* The South African system deprives many people of a fair share in God's earth and society on the basis of racial distinction. Christian change means consultation and participation in decision-making by all, and a redistribution of authority under the kingship of God.

3.4 Caring

Jesus Christ, Saviour, Liberator and Provider, meets in spiritual, mental, and physical needs of people, and has a particular concern for the poor, the outcast, the exploited, and the rejected.

Christians should identify themselves with these sufferers, seeking to help them, and to establish a situation which ensures that need is banished.

* The South African system perpetuates poverty, exploitation, rejection, and deprivation. Many South Africans lack nourishment, housing, education, health services, clothing, and provision for their old age—and people feel no responsibility for it. Chris-

tian change means immediate care for those in need, and a radical change in the structures of society which cause it.

4. THE CHRISTIAN VIEW OF GOVERNMENT

4.1 The Highest Authority

Jesus Christ is the highest authority, and the government of a state is a servant of God and responsible to Him.

Christians should seek to have laws passed which are in accordance with the Gospel of Christ and to urge obedience to them by all citizens.

* Most South African voters give priority to the preservation of white privilege and power and permit the government to use totalitarian methods including detention without trial, bannings, and government by decree. Christian change means the rejection of injustice, the democratic control of all powers of government, equality before the law, the Rule of Law, and a mutual responsibility for making the laws under which men are to be governed.

4.2 The Christian Sphere

God is King of the whole universe, and Jesus Christ entered into all the problems, temptations, and opportunities of human living.

Christians should see all life as a unity of which Christ is the core and the hope.

* Many South Africans divide life into sacred and secular, permitting political opinions and racial attitudes to have ascendancy over Christian criteria in some spheres. Christian change means bringing every facet of life under the Gospel of Jesus Christ.

4.3 The Responsibility to Oppose and Suggest

Jesus Christ, like the prophets before Him and Christians after Him, sought to fulfill God's will even in opposition to the will of people and their rulers.

In proclaiming the good news of Christ, Christians should emulate the example of His followers who defied the unchristian structure or practices of society, and prompted new developments and the solution of social evils.

* The South African social structures incorporate many injustices which prevent the inhabitants from realising the way of Christ. Christians are called to obey God rather than men, even if this involves disobedience to the civil authorities, passive resistance, or defying unchristian laws, and even if the solutions which they suggest are unpopular. Christian change means being willing to change ourselves according to the Gospel.

5. CHRISTIAN UNITY

The one God created Man in His image, and the God-given unity between men is greater than all differences. In Jesus Christ, God creates the one Church as His body on earth.

Christians throughout the world should seek unity in believing, worshipping and serving which transcends all differences of race, culture, and civilisation. They seek that oneness in Christ which is the basis of a common society.

* In South Africa, where the Church is divided into different groups, or divided on racial grounds, or under pressure to support apartheid for political purposes, or to practise discrimination, all Christians should work for Christian unity and support specific efforts of the churches in this regard.

6. CHRISTIAN HOPE

The Creator and Sustainer of the world has a purpose for it which He will fulfil. Jesus Christ reconciles all things and He is the hope of the world.

Christians should have an optimism arising from the grace
of Christ which prompts them to face the blackest circumstances with the assurance of ultimate victory.

* Fear, pessimism, and bitterness dominate the South African scene. Blacks hope for liberation from oppression,
  injustice, and defeat, but the effort to combat fear, the
  heritage of psychological debilitation, and the sheer
  weight of oppression is dismaying. Whites dream of uto-
  pia, snatch at material wealth, but are dominated by fear
  of annihilation. Marginal change is no solution: it pro-
  duces only frustration. Christian change means the discovery of a new verve for living, the courage to proclaim
  fundamental change through the Good News of Jesus
  Christ.

7. THE CHRISTIAN RESPONSE

God loves the world, and enters into its sufferings Himself
in Jesus Christ, making the Cross the way to victory, and
proclaiming in His resurrection that the way to life is the
way of love.

Christians who respond to God's call know that they are
called to take up a cross to follow Him.

* The present South African system can only be maintained by the force of structural violence in opposition to
  God's way. It invites and is threatened by revolutionary
  violence. Christian change means a rapid and radical
  peaceful change towards a society based on the way of
  Christ: love, justice, freedom, truth and responsibility.
  Christians should expect to suffer, to be victorious and to
  call upon all men to respond to God in Jesus Christ.

A Programme of Action for the Christian Institute

1. ROLE

Because it is a living organisation in a developing situation, the Christian Institute needs continually to restate its aims.

1.1 Change

The C.I. is dedicated to help bring change in Southern Africa in the name of Christ. All men should have the opportunity to develop in all fields. This means seeking fundamental change in the attitudes of people, in the structures of power, and in the processes of decision-making.

The C.I. is concerned with reconciliation which means to cast out the fear in our land by love; to banish violence by peacemaking; to shatter despondency and pessimism with joy and hope; to drive out injustice, deceit and oppression with justice, truth and freedom.

The C.I. seeks deep and radical change, in repentance and faith, obedience to the will of God and transformation of society in His name.

1.2 Help

Many organisations are concerned in helping people to live through the apartheid situation. The C.I. shares this concern, but its primary object is to help change the situation. Change and help can be mutually supportive.

1.3 National and International Action

The C.I. recognises that part of its duty is to maintain its witness to a positive Christian answer of love, unity, peace and justice in Southern Africa, on a national and international level.

1.4 Activity

The activity of the C.I. is to encourage groups of people to seek the Way of Christ in the whole experience of living. As individuals they might grow in love, courage and vision, and as a group they might become a living Christian community witnessing to the experience in sharing life's joys and problems.

Christian Change

1. **Christ is Lord**
Renewing human society according to the Gospel of Christ
means personal and national repentance and trust in Christ
for total salvation.

2. **Wholeness**
Bringing every facet of life into obedience to Christ means
rejecting the heresies of racism, apartheid and 'Christian
nationalism.'

3. **Fellowship**
Christian love seeks the unity of all in Christ and the relief
of the needy; it means fundamental changes to laws that
divide and structures that deprive.

4. **Opportunity**
For every human being to develop his potential as a person,
it must be possible for all to share in decision-making and in
the acquisition of land and wealth.

5. **Authority**
Law and government are subject to the Gospel of Christ,
and injustice and totalitarian activities must be rejected;
faced by unchristian laws, Christians should obey God rather
than man.

6. **Ecumenity**
Christians believe, worship and serve in a unity which demands the end of all division and the growth of together-
ness, support and interdependence in all human affairs.

7. **Mission**
The apartheid system is maintained by force against innocent people and it invites revolutionary violence. This way

of life should be radically and peacefully changed towards a life of love and justice in obedience to Christ.

8. Optimism

The pressure of faith, the power of love and the promise of hope challenge and overcome the fear, pessimism and bitterness of the apartheid society of South Africa.

*　　*　　*

This statement on Christian Change is a synopsis of the pamphlet "The Christian Principles for which the Christian Institute stands in Southern Africa."

Statement by
the Christian Institute
on the "Police State" Bills

The Christian Institute Board of Management, at its routine half-yearly meeting today, reaffirmed the Institute's role as a body of followers of Christ, committed to a Christian witness of love and reconciliation in a Society characterised by racial inequalities and divisions, institutionalised violence and the misuse of authoritarian secular power.

In debating the future of the Christian Institute, the Board took note of the terms of proposed legislation to be introduced in the House of Assembly on Monday, as reported by 'Die Transvaler' (16.2. 1974), an official organ of the Nationalist Party.

Since the terms of the proposed new legislation have now been disclosed, we regard it as our urgent duty to comment thereon. The legislation seems to be in two parts, which are closely interlinked.

Firstly, it seems that it is proposed to create quasi-legal machinery to investigate, register and control certain unnamed groups. The Minister of Justice, it appears, will have the power to appoint an "investigatory official" to examine the activities of a "suspected political organisation," with powers of entry, search and interrogation. As a result of his examination the Minister can apparently appoint a committee of enquiry composed of magistrates. It is proposed that severe penalties will be incurred by those who obstruct the investigatory official (R600.00, or one year, or both). On the grounds of the committee's report, the Minister may classify the organisation as "affected." An affected organisation will not be able to solicit, request or receive any monies from abroad. The Minister may also appoint a "Registrar" to "Keep an eye" on such organisations.

Secondly, it is proposed to amend the Riotous Assemblies

Act to restrict even private gatherings, even of two people. A radio announcement will evidently be regarded as sufficient warning. Merely for the Minister or a Chief Magistrate to "fear" that feelings of racial hostility will be incited at a meeting, of whatever nature, will be sufficient reason for it to be forbidden, and indeed for the prohibition to be extended throughout the country. Police will be empowered to set up blockades to prevent attendance at such meetings and they will no longer be required to issue the customary warnings before resorting to force to disperse any such meeting.

In the light of this proposed legislation the Board makes the following comments:

1. The curb on organisations receiving financial assistance from anywhere is a denial of the universality of the Christian Church. We are all members of the same body and no secular authority should have the right to prevent one member from assisting another where there is need.

2. While we cannot regard the C.I. as a "suspect political organisation" it would be naive in the extreme not to see this legislation as inextricably connected with the Schlebusch Commission, which has been investigating the C.I., among others.

3. The C.I. has never made a secret of its commitment to fundamental social change in South Africa in line with the principles of the Gospel. The C.I. is committed to peaceful change. The Government itself, however, endangers peaceful change, which becomes increasingly impossible when the State takes ever more power to suppress, to intimidate and to control the lives and activities of those individuals and groups committed to change.

4. This proposed legislation now removes all doubt that South Africa is a police state. It is a further step in the process of totalitarianism illustrated by the Suppression of Communism Act, the Terrorism Act, the Sabotage Act, the new bill on

censorship, and the systematic use by successive Ministers of Justice of powers arbitrarily to ban, to restrict, and to confine those whom he regards as political opponents.

5. We note that the original recommendation of the Parliamentary Select Committee (later the Schlebusch Commission) to set up a permanent tribunal of enquiry composed of members of Parliament has here been amended in the sense that the "Committee of Enquiry" will be composed of Magistrates. The quasi-judicial appearance of such a committee must not blind us to the fact that real effectiveness lies with the Minister and the quaintly-named officials he will appoint. They are given wide and totally unacceptable powers. This is in fact yet another manifestation of authoritarian, administrative control which helps to clarify the motivations of those who refuse to co-operate with the Schlebusch Commission.

6. We view with abhorrence the yet further invasions of the citizen's privacy and of his rights of association envisaged in the proposed amendment to the Riotous Assemblies Act. The removal of customary and traditional safeguards against abuse of police violence bodies ill for our society.

7. Through this proposed legislation the clash between church and state, between the Christian conscience and the misuse of secular authority becomes yet more apparent and clearly defined. There can be no doubt that the State would not hesitate to use its proposed new powers to interfere in and obstruct the perfectly legitimate activities of Christian individuals and groups seeking to work out the implications of their faith in the socio-political sphere.

8. In view of the serious implications for Christian witness in South Africa, the C.I. calls urgently on all church leaders in the country to express their forthright condemnation of the proposed legislation and to announce unequivocal resistance to any further attempt by the State to encroach on and restrict the activities of the followers of Christ. It calls on individual Christians to prepare themselves for the pain and

suffering which may be the consequence of their resistance to the unacceptable demands of Caesar. We further call on the opposition parties to resist the passing of the proposed legislation with every force at their command.

9. Despite this proposed legislation, the C.I. reaffirms its calm faith in the wisdom and the providence of God, and its sure knowledge that the efforts of rulers to thwart His will are ultimately futile and doomed to failure.

Issued by the Board of Management of the Christian Institute of Southern Africa, 16th February, 1974.

S.A.C.C. Questions Military Violence

The South African Council of Churches took the following resolution on Friday, 2nd August, 1974 at its annual Conference at Hammanskraal. Dr. Douglas Bax proposed the motion and Dr. Beyers Naudé seconded it.

The National Conference of the SACC acknowledges as the one and only God Him who mightily delivered the people of Israel from their bondage in Egypt and who in Jesus Christ still proclaims that He will "set at liberty those who are oppressed" (Luke 4:18). He alone is supreme Lord and Savior and to Him alone we owe ultimate obedience. Therefore "we must obey God rather than men" in those areas where the Government fails to fulfil its calling to be "God's servant for good" rather than for evil and for oppression (Acts 5:29; Romans 13:4).

In the light of this the Conference:

1. Maintains that Christians are called to strive for justice and the true peace which can be founded only on justice:
2. does not accept that it is automatically the duty of those who follow Christ, the Prince of Peace, to engage in violence and war, or to prepare to engage in violence and war, whenever the State demands it:
3. reminds its member Churches that both Catholic and Reformation theology has regarded the taking up of arms as justifiable, if at all, only in order to fight a "just war":
4. points out that the theological definition of a "just war" excludes war in defence of a basically unjust and discriminatory society:
5. points out that the Republic of South Africa is at present a fundamentally unjust and discriminatory society and that this injustice and discrimination constitutes the primary, institutionalised violence which has provoked the counter-violence of the terrorists or freedom fighters:

6. points out that the military forces of our country are being prepared to defend this unjust and discriminatory society and that the threat of military force is in fact already used to defend the status quo against moves for radical change from outside the white electorate:

7. maintains that it is hypocritical to deplore the violence of terrorists or freedom fighters while we ourselves prepare to defend our society with its primary, institutionalised violence by means of yet more violence.

8. points out further that the injustice and oppression under which the black peoples of South Africa labour is far worse than that against which Afrikaners waged their First and Second Wars of Independence and that if we have justified the Afrikaners' resort to violence (or the violence of the imperialism of the English) or claimed that God was on their side, it is hypocritical to deny that the same applies to the black people in their struggle today:

9. questions the basis upon which chaplains are seconded to the military forces lest their presence indicate moral support for the defence of our unjust and discriminatory society.

The Conference therefore:

1. deplores violence as a means to solve problems:

2. calls on its member churches to challenge all their members to consider in view of the above whether Christ's call to take up the Cross and follow Him in identifying with the oppressed does not in our situation involve becoming conscientious objectors:

3. calls on those of its member churches who have chaplains in the military forces to reconsider the basis on which they are appointed and to investigate the state of pastoral care available to the communicants at present in exile or under arms beyond our borders and to seek ways and means of ensuring that such pastoral care may be properly exercised:

4. commends the courage and witness of those who have been willing to go to jail in protest against unjust laws and policies in our land, and who challenge all of us by their example:

5. requests the SACC's task force on Violence and Non-violence to study methods of non-violent action for change which can be recommended to its member churches:

6. prays for the Government and people of our land and urgently calls on them to make rapid strides towards radical and peaceful change in our society so that the violence and war to which our social, economic and political policies are leading us may be avoided.

(*Pro Veritate,* August 1974)

Divine or
Civil Obedience?

Introduction

BECAUSE A believer should always be prepared to give an answer to anyone who calls him to account (1 Peter 3:15), the question must be raised whether it would not be a positive Christian action for people to refuse to cooperate with a Government in a matter which can be proved to be unchristian.

For the purpose of this exposition the appointment by the South African Government of the *"Commission of Inquiry into Certain Organisations"* will serve as well as any other as a general example. For this reason it is used here to illustrate the truth of the gospel which should be valid for all Christians, as we understand it.

1. WHY HAS THE COMMISSION BEEN APPOINTED TO INVESTIGATE THE CHRISTIAN INSTITUTE?

1.1 When the Prime Minister originally suggested in Parliament on 4.2.72 that the Christian Institute among others should be investigated he also said: "Information indicates that there is a *prima facie* case to investigate. Our Parliament must be on the alert for all organisations and currents which do work that undermine. We may not make a mistake in this connection. With such explosive material here South Africa will pay heavily" *Die Transvaler*, 5.2.72). Again on 5.2.72 *Die Transvaler* further reported in connection with the Commission: "Mr. Vorster quoted from the writings of Sir Winston Churchill of 20 years ago, about the *modus operandi* of the Communists in using the banner of freedom to establish a Communist state. These words and this warning of Churchill are still appallingly true today."

Could this mean that the Prime Minister himself prejudiced the Commission and placed it under pressure so that the Commission is now obliged to prove a case against the Christian Institute in order to obviate the Prime Minister's being discredited? "If anyone has prejudged the issue it is the Government itself" (*Sunday Express,* 6.2.72).

Furthermore the National Party and the United Party have also made negative statements about the organisations to be investigated. "The Nationalist Party have already prejudged the issue. There is already a Party commitment on this matter illustrated by the fact that spokesmen of the Nationalist Party have attacked all four organisations on numerous occasions. The Nationalist Party's mind therefore is already made up. When one recalls some of the things the United Party spokesmen have said about Nusas for instance, the same could be said about them" (B. Naudé, T. Kotze—*Sunday Times,* 6.2.72).

Did the Prime Minister's vague references to "Communism," "undermining" and "explosive material" not anticipate the investigation which sprang from the *"prima facie"* case and place pressure on the Commission?

1.2 There is nothing of importance about the Christian Institute (which operates in the open) which the Government does not know already. Seeing that the majority of the politicians who are doing the investigating are Nationalists, the question must be asked whether the inevitable conclusion is not that the Government wishes to make political capital out of the investigation to the detriment of the Christian Institute. "Those of you who thought a Parliamentary Select Committee was impartial and objective will be astounded as I am to learn that Parliamentarians themselves do not think so. Both sides openly attributed bias to the Parliamentary Commission which enquired into the so-called Bell-Herman Martin's sugar scandal" (*Sunday Times,* 16.7.72). One of the members of the Commission itself pleaded for a judicial commission. "Mr. Marais Steyn of Yeoville spoke just before him (the Prime Minister). Earnestly and urgently he asked the Prime Minister rather to appoint a judicial commission" (*Die Vaderland,* 11.2.72).

1.3 It is generally known that the Government is against the existence and the work of the Christian Institute. The Christian Institute witnesses in words and deeds in the name of Christ against the unchristian policy of apartheid, and an alternative to apartheid on all the different social levels of the community has been developed by Spro-cas in its various reports. Seeing that the Prime Minister has apparently classified the Christian Institute as an "undermining" influence, does it not seem that the plan is to balk the Christian Institute in its work? "The mere fact that a Parliamentary Inquiry is being sought by the Prime Minister into the Institute's affairs will be seen by many people as confirmation that the Government is out to silence clergymen who oppose its policies" (*Sunday Express,* 6.2.72).

1.4 The question must be raised whether the fact that the Commission is investigating the Christian Institute together with other organisations means that "guilt by association" can be attached to the Christian Institute. According to a newspaper report it would seem that the Chairman of the Commission not only anticipated the enquiry but prejudged it. *Die Burger* made the following report under the heading: "Probably more shocks says Schlebusch." "There is the possibility that the investigation into the Christian Institute will bring even more shocking things to light than in the case of Wilgespruit, Mr. A.L. Schlebusch, M.P. for Kroonstad and Chairman of the Schlebusch Commission said here yesterday" (*Die Burger,* 24.7.73). Are suspicions possibly raised in this manner against the Christian Institute by association and insinuation? "By linking the Institute of Race Relations with student bodies which do not enjoy a particularly good public image, Mr. Vorster no doubt hopes to smear the Institute and the fourth organisation named, Mr. Beyers Naudé's outspoken and courageous Christian Institute" (*Cape Times,* 8.2.72).

1.5 The work of the Commission led to and resulted in 8 Nusas leaders being severely punished by banning without trial in a court. This means that the investigation by this Commission without the control of normal legal process may result in people being persecuted in an unchristian and unfair manner. Must the conclusion then be drawn that the Christian should not co-operate with a procedure such as this? If he does co-operate he also will be guilty before God because he participated in the process of punishing people in an unchristian manner and persecuting them.

1.6 Is it not clear that the aims in appointing the Commission and the methods of operation prescribed for it, must be questioned in depth in terms of the Gospel?

1.6.1 Jesus said: "Do not judge by appearances but judge with right judgment" (John 7:24).

* Whether the Commission's judgment can be "right" must be questioned. There was supposed to be a *prima facie* case against the Chrstian Institute but we do not even know the nature of the charge, or who the accusers (if any) are.

* The real danger is that the findings of the Commission may already have been prejudiced and placed under pressure by the comments of the Prime Minister and some members of Parliament.

* We are not informed of any accusations against any person or organisation; as a result no right to defence or denial exists and the accusers can never be confronted, challenged or subjected to cross examination.

* The Christian Institute is linked to other organisations and in this manner guilt by association can be attached.

* The members of the Commission are politicians who are bound by certain party policies and as a result they are unlikely to be without prejudice.

* If investigation were necessary—and this we do not believe—it should have been carried out by a judicial commission; the reasonable request for such a commission has been summarily rejected.

1.6.2 Jesus said: "A sound tree cannot bear evil fruit nor can
a bad tree bear good fruit . . . thus you will know them
by their fruit" (Matthew 7:18, 20). The Commission's
work resulted in the Government punishing the Nusas
leaders in an unchristian and unfair manner, without
their having been charged or found guilty in a court of
law. The question must be asked whether one may co-
operate with a procedure which has such results. "So far
six reasons have been given for banning the students
instead of trying them, and none does either the Government or the security system much credit.

Mr. Vorster:	It is unfair to burden the courts with re-sponsibility for security.
	The bannings are preventive not puni-tive.
Mr. Schlebusch:	The students threatened to break the law.
Mr. Pelser:	Trials would give the students a platform.
Mr. Horwood:	Trials would "expose the whole security system."
Mr. L. Nel M.P.:	No time to get the necessary proof for trial.

No one—and not all of these reasons together—justify
abuse of the rule of law" (*The Star,* 27.3.73).

2. THE COMMISSION'S METHOD OF OPERATION

2.1 The mandate of the Commission requires that its work be
done in secret.

Jesus said: "For everyone who does evil hates the light and
does not come to the light lest his deeds should be exposed. He
who does what is true comes to the light that it may be clearly
seen that his deeds have been wrought in God" (John 3:20–21).

Do the following implications of the Gospel of Christ not
apply to the Christian Institute, the Government and also to the
Commission?

"The Church lives from the disclosure of the true God and

His revelation, from Him as the Light that has been lit in Jesus Christ to destroy the works of darkness. It lives in the dawning of the day of the Lord and its task in relation to the world is to rouse it and tell it that this day has dawned. The inevitable political corollary of this is that the Church is *the sworn enemy of all secret policies and secret diplomacy. It is just as true of the political sphere as of any other that only evil can want to be kept secret.* The distinguishing mark of good is that it presses forward to the light of day. Where freedom and responsibility in the service of the State are one, whatever is said and done must be said and done before the ears and eyes of all, and the legislator, the ruler and the judge can and must be ready to answer openly for all their actions.

The Statecraft that wraps itself up in darkness is the craft of a State which, because it is anarchic or tyrannical, is forced to hide the bad conscience of its citizens or officials. The church will not on any account lend its support to that kind of State" (Epitome of: CHRISTENGEMEINDE UND BÜRGER-GEMEINDE, Prof. Karl Barth; our italics). This means that right and righteousness must not only be done, but must also be *seen* by everybody to be done.

Because the investigation takes place in secret, there is abundant scope for false evidence and damage to the good name of Christians. The ninth commandment says: "You shall not give false witness against your neighbour." According to the Nederduitse Gereformeerde Doctrine this means "that I do not judge, or join in condemning, any man rashly or unheard . . . and that, as far as I am able, I defend and promote the honour and reputation of my neighbour" (*CATECHISM,* answer 112).

2.2 Is the freedom of the people who give evidence, not curtailed because they are sworn to secrecy? Does it not clash in a similar way with the following implication of the Gospel of Christ?

"The Church sees itself established and nourished by the free Word of God—the Word which proves its freedom in the Holy Scriptures at all times. And the Church believes that the human word is capable of being the free vehicle and mouthpiece of this free Word of God. *It will do all it can to see that there are opportunities for mutual discussion in the civil community as the basis of common endeavours. And it will try to see that such discussion takes place openly.* With all its strength it will be on the side of those who refuse to have anything to do with the regimentation, controlling and censoring of public opinion. It knows of no pretext which would make that a good thing and no situation in which it could be necessary" (*op. cit.,* Prof. Karl Barth; our italics).

2.3 Does the Commission not deviate from the normal, acknowledged legal procedures of democracy and is it not true that in so doing it diverges from the rule of law? Normally this means that the three usual functions, namely the legislative, the judicial and the executive power are attached to three different groups. Here the powers entrusted to the Commission include not only the legislative but also the judicial aspects.

"Since the Church is aware of the variety of the gifts and tasks of the one Holy Spirit in its own sphere, it will be alert and open in the political sphere to the need to separate the different functions and 'powers'—the legislative, executive and the judicial—inasmuch as those who carry out any one of these functions should not carry out the others simultaneously. *No human is a god able to unite in his own person the functions of the legislator and the ruler, the ruler and the judge, without endangering the sovereignty of the law*" (op. cit., Prof. K. Barth; our italics). R. Wessler confirms this truth: "The democratic State has definite indispensable characteristic features. To this belongs the division of the power of state in (a) legislation, (b) government, (c) justice, which should be separated as far as possible" (*SOCIAL ETHICS,* p. 142).

So long as the *modus operandi* of the commission does not adhere to the usual rule of law of a democracy, neither the individual nor the Christian Institute organisation is protected by the accepted legal procedures. The question must be asked whether this does not expose those who appear before the Commission to possible errors of judgment by this authority.

Are not certain indispensable elements inherent in the rule of law, elements which the Commission must of necessity ignore? ". . . that every person whose interest will be affected by a judicial or administrative decision has the right to a meaningful 'day in court'; that deciding officers shall be independent in the full sense, free from external direction by political and administrative superiors in the disposition of individual cases and inwardly free from the influences of personal gain and partisan or popular bias"—A.W. Jones as quoted by Prof. A.S. Mathews, *LAW, ORDER AND LIBERTY IN S.A.,* p. 15. And further: "The inevitability of human error . . . requires that the law, and the assumptions which underlie it, should be interpreted by a judiciary which is as far as possible independent of the Executive and the Legislature" (Report of the Fourth Committee, *THE RULE OF LAW IN A FREE SOCIETY,* p. 279, quoted by A.S. Mathews, op. cit. on p. 45).

The normal legal process protects the basic rights of the individual and limits the power of the governing body in order that it will not become arbitrary power. Is it not clear therefore, that because it by-passes the rule of law and the usual democratic legal procedures, the commission is in a position to violate justice, basically? If this happens, its power will not be the "potestas" which adheres to the law and serves it, but will become "potentia" (power for the sake of power), which forestalls justice and subjects it, bends it, and breaks it. This type of authority in itself of necessity becomes evil: "Notwithstanding their arbitrariness, power and justice are mutually adjoined sides of the God-maintained and ordained existence of man" (*MACHT UND RECHT,* H. Dombois und E. Wilkins, p. 200).

The warning must be heard: "He who takes up the sword shall perish by the sword." He who employs absolute power shall be destroyed thereby. (Power corrupts and absolute power corrupts absolutely.)

2.4 The Commission's investigation resulted in the Nusas leaders being punished by the Government, arbitrarily and harshly, by way of banning without trial. As opposed to this the Gospel of Jesus Christ must be stated:

"Jesus answered him. 'If I have spoken wrongly, bear witness to the wrong; but if I have spoken rightly, why do you strike me?' (John 18:23)." This means that if there has been wrongdoing according to God's will, then it must be proved openly and punishment can be meted out. If, however the evil is not proved in public, there may not be "striking", banning or punishment. Whosoever does this, does it to Christ himself. ". . . none of our brothers may be hurt, despised, rejected, misused or offended in any manner by us, without at the same time hurting, despising and misusing Christ through the wrong things that we do . . . we should care for the bodies of our brothers as for our own" (*INSTITUTION IV*, 8, J. CALVIN).

3. THE RIGHT AND THE DUTY TO RESIST UN-CHRISTIAN GOVERNMENTAL AUTHORITY IN THE NAME OF CHRIST

The believer in Christ not only has the right, but the responsibility to hearken to the Word of God and His righteousness rather than to the government, should the government deviate from God's will. Does not the responsibility lie with the Christian not to co-operate with the government in a matter which is in conflict with the Gospel? By doing so is he not witnessing to Christ and his righteousness?

Civil disobedience is an act of protest by the Christian on the grounds of Christian conscience. It is only permissible when authority expects of him an unchristian deed and pleas for a return to observance of the Gospel have not availed. "The right of passive resistance can only be applied if it becomes apparent that no other method can overcome the emergency situation and restore righteousness" (*DIE STRYD OM DIE ORDES*, Prof. H.G. Stoker, p. 243). The State and its commissions do have authority over the citizens, but in a moral sense the individual has a personal right towards the State for inasmuch as the citizen is part of the structure of the State, he is subject to the authority of the State; as a person before God even within the structures of the State he is however, totally subject to God. "In the last instance the Christian may not be bound by the State's authority because it is not the final dominion of God and therefore belongs to the being of the historical world which passes (*GLAUBE IN POLITISCHE ENTSCHEIDUNG*, Dr. A. Rich, p. 161). Man never belongs totally to the State. He cannot be degraded into being a pawn of the State; the State exists for the benefit of man, not man for the benefit of the State.

Is it possible that the powers granted to this commission by the Government and the results flowing from it reveal a totalitarian tendency? A totalitarian State usually wants complete control over its subjects. "Its conflict with the Church is therefore not a coincidence, but is inevitable for as long as the Church remains a Church which knows the absolute necessity of its inner independence. Such a State can tolerate the inner independence of the Church even less than its outward independence, because it wants to control the soul of man. It is the soul that it wishes to control and shape after its own image" (*GERECHTIGHEIT*, Prof. E. Brunner, p. 216).

It must be remembered that the most important matter for the citizens of a democratic state is not blind *obedience* and servile *submissiveness* to the Government, but joint responsibility for the concerns of State in the sight of God. "Democracy strives to curtail the freedom of the individual as little as possible but that freedom must result in maintaining the joint responsibility" (Wessler, op. cit. p. 142). Cf. also Wolfgang Trillhaas: "Accordingly obedience is no longer the predominant problem of the citizen. Much more is it the responsibility (or the joint responsibility) for the success of the State in the political life" (*ETHIK*, Wolfgang Trillhaas, p. 373).

It must also be remembered what Reinhold Niebuhr said about the Christian motivation of democracy, namely, that human strivings towards justice make democracy possible, but the human inclination towards injustice makes democracy *essential*.

It may be that this type of action on the part of the Government reveals tendencies towards fascism, and such a Government then no longer *serves* but *dominates*. In such a situation the tendency is to govern by means of arbitrary power and to control by force. Government becomes primarily a power structure. If such a Government continues in this headlong way, the logical outcome is that it becomes idolatrous because everything has to flow out of, through and towards the National State. (cf. Revelation 13). The Government's task is *not* to create arbitrary law. Its task is to reduce to writing in the form of legislation the substantive will of God as revealed in the Gospel. A Government with fascist leanings, however, creates its own justice which it enforces by way of penal sanctions. Anything opposed to the will or policy of such a Government is then regarded as subversive or as dangerous to the State. Freedom is regarded as a concession from the Government and not the normal way of life. In this the Government as well as the Commission will have to answer to God in regard to the bannings and also in regard to punishment which may possibly follow for those who refuse on grounds of conscience to testify before the Commission.

The power of a State such as this is not only territorial and military but also moral. As a result everything has to be subjected to the authoritarian, co-operative State—nothing is outside its power and authority and it determines the norms, even in relation to conscience. As a result a person may be led to violate his conscience, make it conformable and sacrifice it to the State. "The more sensitive such a conscience is and the more receptive to the will of God, the more dangerous it is to offer it in sacrifice. He who is more obedient to man than to God against his better judgment and his conscience, destroys the integrity of his being, his unity within himself, and sooner or later he falls victim to schizophrenia" (*FREIHEIT UND BINDUNG DES CHRISTEN IN DER POLITIK,* T. Ellwyn, p. 27).

In this kind of State the real issue at stake is not whether the Government is *right or wrong, good or bad,* but whether the order, the policy and the will of the State, *fails or succeeds.*

If the present Government, as shown incidentally by the appointment of this Commission, reveals the abovementioned traits, should it not be called back to the Gospel of Christ? If we too are guilty, the same applies to us. If such a call is ineffectual

". . . it becomes a matter of a clash between religious belief and Government, a clash in which man should be obedient to God rather than to the person in authority . . ." (Prof. H.G. Stoker, op. cit. p. 243). The believer can, however, only act outside the law and refuse to co-operate if he acts according to God's will which is being violated by authority. "Without justification nobody should claim the 'right' to offer resistance against the authorities. This justification should in my opinion, include the responsibility of resistance and must be included with the 'Higher Authority' in whose name you are acting" (*ETHIK*, Wolfgang Trillhaas, p. 373).

When reading Romans 13:1 "Let every person be subject to the governing authorities . . ." it must be remembered that the Government does not have authority and power just because it is the Government as such, but because it is "God's servant" (verse 4). "The problem about the right to resist . . . is in fact contained in Romans 13. We ought to consider whether the term 'God's servant' does not include the right to resist when the authorities exceed their God-given mandate and turn away from the clearly articulated commandments of God" (W. Schulze, quoted in *POLITIK SWISCHEN DäMON UND GOTT*, Dr. W. Kunneth, p. 301). Authority is only legitimate when it does not act contrary to God's will.

The same thought was expressed in the 1973 Studies of the Christian Institute as follows: ". . . the concept of the Government of a country as a creation and system of God in itself, is false and a Government is always subject to the righteousness of the Gospel. 'It is exegetically no longer possible to base obedience to Governments on some peculiar character in them' " (H.W. Bartsch).

Peter 2:13 'Be submitted to every human ordinance because of the Lord' must be correctly translated as 'Be subject to everyone (every human creature) for the Lord's sake' (H.W. Bartsch).

The words in Romans 13: 'The Government is ordained by God' and 'they are servants (ministers) of God' do not refer to a peculiar commission or dignity of the Government but to what it in fact is, whether it accepts Romans 13 or not. God did not give special commission to the Government as such. The trend therefore, is to *"debunk the false concept of Govern-ments"* (*POVERTY IN ABUNDANCE OR ABUNDANCE IN POVERTY?,* Roelf Meyer, p. 13).

Where such deviation from the Gospel occurs, it is therefore not only the right of the Christian to resist authority, but his duty to offer passive resistance in obedience to the Gospel, even if in so doing he has to disobey the Government. If a Govern-ment violates the Gospel, it loses its authority to be obeyed in its office as ruler. "The Government loses its essential office because of its contradictory attitude towards God" (W. Kunneth, op. cit., p. 294). And: "As an extension of these thoughts the right, even the duty can be imposed on the subject to resist the tyrant who commits an act of violence against a private person by the misuse of his office" (W. Kunneth, op. cit., p. 295).

Therefore one can only speak of Government and its author-ity ". . . as long as it is said that it possesses the intention and the capability to accept responsibility for justice and righteous-ness: If this governmental function is distorted, however, then that Government has dissolved itself, its authority is no longer from God, and it is plainly in conflict with God. As a result of this, according to Romans 13, the Christian is no longer re-quired to be obedient to the guilty (Government), but to a much greater extent obliged to resist such a Government which has degenerated" (W. Kunneth, op. cit., p. 301).

The Calvinist, John Knox, also advocates the same idea. In his ". . . conversations with Queen Mary he had declared not only the right of the nobility to resist in defence of the people but the right of the subject to disobey where the ruler contra-venes the law of God" (*CALVINISM AND THE POLITICAL ORDER,* G.L. Hunt, p. 14). Calvin championed this same truth in vigorous language: "Because earthly princes forfeit all their power when they revolt against God . . . We should resist them rather than obey . . ." *(LECTURE XIII).*

The authority of the Government and State as such is not rejected in general by these ideas but maintained, because it is still *de facto* the Government, even if it deviates in essential points from the Gospel and then it has to be resisted. "Even a distorted governmental system still retains the remnants and elements of the stable order of God" (W. Kunneth, op. cit., p. 302).

A step such as this of disobeying the Government, must be taken on grounds of Christian conscience. The Christian's conscience is that God-given ability to distinguish between right and wrong according to the criterion of the Gospel, which inwardly compels him to follow the right course. ". . . Conscience also has the remarkable result that it can suddenly initiate resistance against the Government; an inner distress can also make itself felt when he allows the Government to force him to commit acts which he knows to be wrong." Paul experiences a similar distress in Romans 9:1,2 (*CHRISTELIJKE ENCYCLOPEDIE DEEL III,* Prof. H. Schippers, p. 218). Conscience is the inner will that urges one to respond to the conscious norms, and the Christian conscience is bound up with the Gospel.

When the Government deviates from the Gospel, the Christian is bound by his conscience to resist it. Even if this results in breaking the law, it has to be done because God's will must be maintained above the law of man (Acts 4). The Government is God's servant and this means that it cannot arbitrarily place itself above the rule of law without impinging on the highest authority. If it does it, it becomes the evil-doer, (Romans 13) which must be resisted in obedience to God.

4. CHRISTIANS MAY IN PRAYERFUL ANTICIPATION HOPE

Christians may in prayerful anticipation hope that a Government which does not conform to the Gospel with regard to a particular matter may be brought to 're-think' its attitude. They hope for even more; namely, that God's righteousness may become the criterion in every facet of their lives, and particularly in their political life in South Africa. For this they work and pray.

If, however the Government persecutes a Christian who finds it impossible to co-operate when departure from the Gospel occurs, the pertinent question must be asked: What is the crime against Christ for which he has to be punished? For this the Government would have to supply an answer to God and to South Africa. The Government, already persecuting and punishing people in an unchristian manner, must remember that when Saul persecuted some believers, Christ asked him: "Saul, Saul, why do you persecute *Me*?" (Acts 9:4). Is it not the duty of a Christian in such a situation constantly and in deep humility to call his fellowmen to the same obedience in the light of the Gospel? And should a Christian not appeal to the Government in terms of the Gospel to turn away from its wrong course? "Repent . . . even now the axe is laid to the root of the trees; every tree therefore that does not bear good fruit is cut down and thrown into the fire" (Matthew 3).

Those who are involved in refusing to testify to the "Commission of Inquiry into Certain Organisations," (used here as a general example), wish to repeat that they have nothing to hide and that, if an investigation is deemed necessary (an opinion with which they would not concur), they would be willing to testify to and co-operate with a public, impartial, judicial court of enquiry.

In refusing to testify and co-operate with the Government in a matter such as this, those who cannot co-operate on grounds of their Christian conscience do not wish to pose as heroes or martyrs, (as a section of the Afrikaans press has implied); they are concerned about obedience to Christ, the highest authority.

The signatories wish to remain faithful to Christ, by the grace of God because:

VERBUM DEI MANET IN AETERNUM.

Issued by:
Brian Brown, Theo Kotzé, Roelf Meyer, Beyers Naudé and J.E. Phakathi.

Reinhold Niebuhr Award For 1974 To Dr. C.F.B. Naudé—Citation

Churchamn, Pastor, Prophet, and Therefore Risk-Taker on Behalf of Others;

Affirmer of the Lordship of Christ, and Therefore Denier of The Lordship of Caesar;

Believer in God's Love, and Therefore Practitioner of Human Justice;

Provider of Space for Total Sharing, and Therefore Troubler of the *Status Quo;*

Exemplar of a Courage that Challenges Others to Risk More Because He Continually Risks All.

Christian Involvement in the Struggle For Human Rights and Justice

(Reply of Beyers Naudé in response to the Reinhold Niebuhr Award.)

Man's search for truth is a long and tortuous one and the discovery thereof has usually been preceded by much agony and struggle of mind, body and spirit. In fact, when looking at history, it seems such discovery and expression of truth is inseparable from a measure of sacrifices, greater or smaller, according to the nature and duration of the struggle. It is also true to state that many times the forces of religion, including the Christian religion, viewed with alarm efforts to discover truth and even played a leading role in opposing and resisting such efforts, claiming that they would seriously threaten the traditional religious or doctrinal beliefs which were currently held. This viewpoint portrayed the lack of awareness that no power on earth can permanently prevent the discovery and advancement of truth. Another fact which leaders of Christian churches failed many times to realise was that the message of the Christian faith as presented through the Old and New Testaments contains within itself the seed of the most powerful force for the renewal and transformation of human life and human society imaginable.

The absence of this understanding and awareness has been one of the main reasons why, in the long struggle of the human race to establish and ensure human rights, the institutionalised church has time and again failed to become involved in such struggles—or if it eventually did, many times only belatedly. It would also be true to state—and I say this with deep regret—that in a number of instances the Christian Church actively sided with the ecclesiastical, political, social or economic status quo, and even went further by actively opposing and rejecting the efforts of those who were deeply concerned to achieve social justice and full human rights for oppressed individuals and communities. Examples abound where the Church initiated, blessed, and supported forms of warfare it regarded as justified violence in the defence of honourable causes; where the Church gathered material riches in abundance and excess for itself amidst abject poverty, hunger, and distress; where the Church remained silent at organized as well as unorganized forms of oppression of millions of people; where the Church either approved, supported, or compromised itself through its silence in protesting and acting against inhuman systems such as slavery.

It is equally true, however, that from the ranks of this same institution has emerged a continuous stream of individuals and groups which, over a long stretch of time, have become involved in the struggle for human rights in a spirit of courage, perseverance, and sacrifice which has astounded many, which has given hope to millions, and brought about fundamental and lasting reform.

How does one account for this strange phenomenon of conflicting forces within the same body, where the official institution seems unwilling or incapable of facing the challenge of political and social justice whilst at the same time giving birth to powerful forces and movements which create the very challenge which the Church itself is afraid or unable to face?

There are many reasons which could be given for this historic phenomenon: I only wish to advance the following two which seem to me to be relevant to our concern for human rights in the world today:

1. The first is the lack of understanding of the Biblical concept of man as created in the image of God. For many centuries the institutionalised Church was unable, because of the theological interpretation it held regarding the concept of authority—the authority of God, of the Church, of the State, and of the individual—to discover the concept of man as a person created in the image of God, and endowed with inalienable rights in the sight of God. It was only when new political developments in the last decades forced nations to face the issue of fundamental human rights, especially after the Second World War, that the institutionalised Church was challenged to indicate and define its understanding. Even then, it took many decades of shocking violations of such rights in many parts of the world before church bodies started to speak out on this issue. Such expression of conviction initially was made by individual groups of Christians who found themselves living under systems of severe repression, oppression, or tyranny, and were thereby challenged to the depths of their beings. The Barmen Declaration in the time of the Nazi regime is an eminent example of such conviction when it stated:

    We reject the false doctrine, as though the State, over and beyond its special commission, should and could become the single and totalitarian order of human life, thus fulfilling the Church's vocation as well.

    Another more recent and deeply moving example is the Theological Declaration of Korean Christians, 1973, which, in defining Christian responsibility under a repressive society, states as follows:

    World power is entrusted by God to civil authority to keep justice and order in human society. If any people pose themselves above the law and betray the divine mandate for justice, they are in rebellion against God.

In the same spirit a group of Christians in South Africa which refused to testify before a governmental commission of inquiry called the Schlebusch Commission in 1973, because of its secrecy in operations and its lack of judicial impartiality, stated as follows:

When the Government deviates from the Gospel, the Christian is bound by his conscience to resist it, even if this results in breaking the law. It has to be done because God's will must be maintained above the law of men. (Acts 4) The Government is God's servant and this means that it cannot arbitrarily place itself above the rule of law without impinging on the highest authority. If it does so, it becomes the evil-doer, (Romans 13) which must be resisted in obedience to God.

And as recently as October 13, 1974, the National Council of the Churches of Christ in the USA adopted a resolution on human rights, the introductory paragraph of which reads as follows:

Respect for human rights lies at the very heart of our Christian faith. All persons are created in the image of God and are endowed with the freedom to mirror in their relationship to God, labor, nature, and society the divine intention for a harmony of love, justice and peace.

2.   The second reason I wish to mention is the confusion found within the institutionalized Church to understand the nature of social evil, especially as it expresses itself in forms of violence and of the inability of the Church to draw even upon spiritual and moral resources which it claims to possess in order to counteract such evil by other than violent means.

For centuries the vast majority of clergy and laity in the church thought of violence mainly in terms of physical force or pain. The other many and varied, more subtle and sophisticated, but therefore not less threatening, painful, humiliating, and dehumanising forms of violence which the human family has devised, sanctioned, and implemented—such as gross political injustice, economic exploitation, psychological terror, or socially destructive systems—these have taken many centuries to be designated as forms of violence equally unacceptable, equally and even more destructive than physical violence was usually judged to be.

Today not only the Church as institution but also governments, nations, and human beings in their millions are being confronted by the spectre of violence in many of the forms mentioned above. One senses that the wide spectrum of conflict has left many people with a deep sense of confusion, fear and despair, with the most dangerous emotion being that of a deep spiritual inertia which seems to have taken hold of large sections of the human family because of the feeling of helplessness in relation to any meaningful resolution of the threat to human rights being found except through other forms of violence.

This is one of the crucial questions with which the Christian Church and the Christian community throughout the world is faced, together with all the inhabitants of the globe. Deep differences of conviction are being held and expressed on this issue not only within but also outside the organized Church. One is constantly reminded of the fact that long-existing situations and systems of oppression and violence called into being struggles where counter-violence was seen to be the inevitable answer to meet and overcome such existing forms of violence, and I do not think that Christ gives us the right to judge or condemn those who, in finding themselves in such situations of tyranny and oppression, have come to the conclusion that, having tried all else, there is no option left to procure liberation but through violence. But I hold the conviction that this is not, cannot be, and will never be the truly satisfying answer which God has made available to his children on earth. I sense—and I admit to my inadequacy or failure in grasping this more clearly—that there is a dimension of divine power and moral force available to us as human beings which we as a Church or as a Christian community have not yet been able to grasp and act upon. In the tradition of such great men as Mahatma Gandhi and Martin Luther King, I implicitly believe that once this divine power of moral force is understood and fully and effectively utilized, it will in turn create a human initiative presently lacking in our society to resolve situations and systems of conflict through other means than those of violence.

One of the essential elements which would be required to operate in order to allow this moral force to display itself is that of voluntary individual or communal suffering on the part of those involved in the struggle for human dignity and human rights. I believe that the Christian community throughout the world needs to reflect much more deeply on the nature of suffering, especially as it has been exemplified through the life and death of Christ, in order to give a more satisfying answer than the Christian community has done up till the present day.

May I now turn for a moment to South Africa, the land of my birth and of my love. For many decades, long before whites spoke out, voices of concern and protest had been raised by black leaders in our country against the oppressive system of apartheid, the most well-known of such voices being that of Albert Luthuli, whose consistent pleas for non-violent change, in which he was joined by many others, have been largely ignored by our white community. In 1963 a small body of deeply concerned Christians of all races and denominations in South Africa (called the Christian Institute of Southern Africa) started to join forces with the voices of protest and the pleas for fundamental, peaceful change. During the last eleven years our aims have been ridiculed, our activities have been made suspect, our pleas and warnings have been largely ignored by the majority of the white community of our country. And even when, through fear of being publicly identified with us, a number of whites have privately conceded that the Christian principles regarding human dignity and human rights which we proclaim and try to implement cannot be faulted, the customary criticism against us was always one of too great haste. (Significantly, I have not heard of a single black using this argument!)

It would have been much easier for the white members in the Christian Institute to continue to enjoy all the privileges of an unjust society which by its very nature discriminates in favour of whites; it would have been so much easier for the black members of the Institute to give up in anger, bitterness, or despair; it would have been possible to retaliate in hatred or even to turn to forms of counter-violence. We did none of these: whatever mistakes we may have made we left nobody, either inside or outside our country, in doubt as to where we stand and why we stand there. We are committed to the recognition of the dignity and the fundamental rights of every human being, regardless of race, colour, creed or sex; we are committed, in accordance with our understanding of the Christian faith, to do everything in our power to achieve these goals by peaceful means; we are committed to the task of reconciliation based on justice and of Christian liberation through justice without which no lasting reconciliation could be procured.

We do not know whether we will succeed—at the present moment it seems more likely that we might fail—but the real and lasting test of success or failure is not always determined by visible signs. Your recognition of our struggle through the honour you have bestowed upon me is in itself a tremendous source of encouragement and hope. But it is also a recognition of the belief which we strongly hold that because this earth is God's earth, such rights must be accorded to all God's children everywhere on this globe.

May I close by quoting part of a soliloquy recently written by John Harriott, a Jesuit priest of Britain, which so meaningfully expresses the hope of the Christian faith which has inspired our efforts in South Africa:

Let us open the clenched fist and extend the open palm
Let us mourn till others are comforted, weep till others laugh
Let us be sleepless till all can sleep untroubled
Let us be meek till all can stand up in pride
Let us be frugal till all are filled
Let us give till all have received
Let us make no claims till all have had their due
Let us be slaves till all are free
Let us lay down our lives till others have life abundantly.

(*Pro Veritate*, January 1975)

Statement by
Dr. Beyers Naudé
Director of the Christian Institute
Made on 28.5.75 on Behalf of
the Board of Management

The Report of the Le Grange Commission has, according to press reports, made allegations about the Christian Institute which I am bound to refute.

1. With regard to the use of violence as an instrument of social change, the reported allegation that the institute advocates the use of violence in private while publicly opposing its use is utterly untrue. The affairs and action of the C.I. have always been open to anyone, and there is no dichotomy between its private and public policies. The C.I. has no secrets, and has consistently advocated Christian change by non-violent means.

2. It is alleged that the C.I. supports the aims of the World Council of Churches with regard to "violent action against the Republic in the form of assistance to terrorist organizations."

We wish to confirm the statement made by Mr. Fred van Wyk, Chairman of the C.I.'s Board of Trustees, that the C.I. does not receive financial support from the WCC. All the C.I.'s overseas funds are contributed directly by churches and Christian agencies from various countries. The fact that some of these bodies also contribute directly to WCC funds is their own independent action, as is their support of the C.I.'s projects. We just further point out that the C.I. has received grants from South African churches who are also members of the WCC. Many other churches have received aid from the same overseas sources as the C.I. has. The fact that the truthful evidence of this witness was summarily rejected by the Commission is ample proof of the biased way in which facts were selected to suit a predetermined judgment.

3. The C.I.'s consistent and public standpoint has been to

advocate justice through reconciliation. This standpoint was always followed by the Spro-cas II project, a fact which makes nonsense of the Commission's allegations that the Spro-cas planners tried to substitute the present order with a "Black-dominated socialist system" through racial conflict and by "engineering a revolution." These baseless accusations totally discredit the findings of the commission as reported by the press.

4. Radical change is a biblical concept—one which was fundamental to the Christian Gospel long before any formulation of Marxist or Neo-Marxist doctrines. The use of this kind of political jargon is a crude and unsuccessful attempt to smear the C.I.

5. The nature of the report confirms our previous conviction that those who refused to testify before the Commission were fully justified in their stand.

A Statement from Dr. Beyers Naudé and Prof. C. Gardner
of the Board of Management of the Christian Institute 29.5.75

A reading of the Le Grange Commission's Report on the Christian Institute reveals clearly that it is a patchwork of outright lies, half-truths and facts taken out of context.

Furthermore, the Report deals entirely with the ideas and beliefs of the C.I. and related organisations and reveals no evidence of any action which could be regarded as subversive or designed to overthrow the State by violence. The C.I. is prepared to face any allegations in an open court.

The central premise of the Report is "the generally accepted principle that the supreme authority which has its origin in the juridical sphere is vested in the State." This is naked totalitarianism which claims the God-given right over the total life of man, and which the C.I. utterly rejects.

We cannot deplore strongly enough the role of those anonymous theologians who have lent themselves to the Commission's false political interpretations of relevant theology.

Attempting to limit the witness of Christians in this way constitutes a grave threat to the prophetic role of the Church.

A service of dedication to Christ and the work of the C.I. in his name is being planned for Sunday afternoon, June 1st, at a venue to be announced later.

(Pro Veritate, June 1975)

Statements on Detentions

JAMES POLLEY

Our friend and colleague, the Rev. James Polley, a member of this National Board of Management of the Christian Institute, has been detained under the Terrorism Act.

This barbaric law makes it possible for the police to hold a citizen without trial for an indefinite length of time, without access to loved ones or legal advice.

We are appalled by the action that has been taken against James and against all others who are being held under these so-called security laws which provide for indefinite detention without trial. We stand by James Polley particularly, whom we know as a friend and a Christian minister.

State action of this kind affects every citizen. Where Christians are acted against in this way for standing up for Christian principles it is the church which is being attacked.

If a major purpose of this kind of action is to put fear into the hearts of citizens, as we believe is the case, these actions under the Terrorism Act itself amount to nothing less than acts of terrorism and provoke counter-violence.

We call for the repeal of the Terrorism Act, and for the immediate release of James Polley and all prisoners who are being detained without trial in this country, or for them to be brought to trial under laws which do not contravene principles of justice.

We call, too, for a public assurance from the Minister of Justice that nobody held under any law in any gaol or police station will be physically or mentally maltreated in any way.

—*Board of Management of the Christian Institute, 5.9.75.*

HORST KLEINSCHMIDT

This marks a further disgraceful episode in South Africa's sorry recent history. It is obvious the Government will tolerate no opposition in its march towards totalitarianism. To those of us who know Horst well, there seems to be no other reason for his detention but that he has been of tremendous practical assistance to the families of detainees. His compassion is an example to us all.

The work will go on. Neither the Affected Organizations Act nor actions against staff members will prevent the Christian Institute carrying on its prophetic and reconciling work.

—Theo Kotzé, 16th September, 1975

***

The Christian Institute today pledged its total support and solidarity for Mr. Horst Kleinschmidt, who was detained under the Terrorism Act today.

Mr. Horst Kleinschmidt is a former youth organiser of the Progressive Party.

A statement issued today by the CI director, Dr. Naudé, and the Rev. Roelf Meyer, editor of *Pro Veritate*, the CI's journal, attacked the detention of Mr. Kleinschmidt and condemned the Terrorism Act.

Dr. Naudé said: "Through our concern to assist families of detained people, we have come to know something about the agony caused by this system of detention without trial.

"But now that one of the Christian Institute members has been taken in, we realise more than ever the tremendous repressive powers which this Act imparts to the Security Police."

(*Pro Veritate*, October 1975)

Parliamentary
Internal Security Commission Bill

This meeting of the Board of Management of the Christian Institute has taken note of the proposed legislation for a Parliamentary Internal Security Commission. This Bill comes as no surprise as it is a logical outcome of the powers given to the Schlebusch Le Grange Commission. It is also in line with numerous other forms of legislation which claim to be concerned with peace and order but which in fact promote tension and disorder and violate the Christian concept of justice.

It is a political measure which seeks to increase the fear and insecurity amongst white voters so that they will permit, excuse and expect the government's use of totalitarian powers to subjugate the majority of our citizens who have no legitimate means of political expression. As a result it subverts rather than promotes the real security of our country which we so deeply desire.

This legislation will inevitably lead to a process of moral disintegration and the corruption of relationships of trust between individuals and groups. The state of suspicion thus created destroys the very basis on which any stable and secure society should be built and maintained, and for these reasons we totally reject this Bill.

As Christians in South Africa we share in the responsibility and in the guilt for this destructive process, which has already caused untold suffering. We foresee that injustice, oppression and the erosion of human freedom will increase. Through the times of peril which lie ahead Christians are called upon to accept suffering as the price of obedience to God's demands for justice and reconciliation.

We build our hope and trust for the future on God's promise and commit ourselves to continue to pray and work for justice and Christian liberation in Southern Africa.

Johannesburg, February 21st., 1976.

(Pro Veritate, March 1976)

Foreign Investment in South Africa

A statement by
Chief Gatsha Buthelezi and
Dr. C.F. Beyers Naudé.

A radical redistribution of wealth, land and political power is essential for the establishment of a stable and moral society in South Africa.

In South Africa for over a century capitalistic paternalism has produced the conclusive evidence which makes us reject government by minority elite. Men have been consistently dehumanised, the many blatantly crushed to produce wealth for the few, and the whole of society designed to protect and intensify this naked exploitation of man by man.

We are convinced that this capitalistic endeavour is doomed. It will fail because the selfishness of South Africa's White elite is already unrealistic and cannot survive in today's world. It will fail because the needy millions of South Africa require for themselves the liberation they witness amongst their brothers in neighbouring states. It will fail because no "concessions" can relax the grip of capitalistic control enough to enable the oppressed masses to discover and express their own dignity and self-respect in our land.

Within this framework we must respond to the following statement by the Hon. M.C. Botha, Minister of Bantu Administration and Development.

> . . . In the economic framework of the country, the economy of the homelands is interwoven with that of the Republic and it stands to reason that the development of the homelands cannot be carried out at a pace which would have a detrimental effect on the economy of the country. . . .

If the Homelands exist to make labour available to maintain the cash economy and standard of living of the elite (Black, White or both) and to establish an economic buffer zone of homeland economies to protect the central economy and provide benefits for the favoured few, we can come to only one conclusion. Foreign investment in the central economy is devoid of all morality.

It is equally evident that attempts to increase the responsibility of employers and investors within this system will do nothing to produce the radical redistribution of wealth and power which are the essential prerequisites of justice and peace. Nor can professional economists in theoretical debate produce a relevant solution. Progress depends on realising the priorities and power locked in the wisdom of the Black man who has suffered and will survive to make the real contribution to the new society which he is seeking.

Whites in South Africa have denied Blacks access to the central parliamentary decision-making process. They have imposed on Blacks a divide and rule policy as though the Blacks of the country have no right to speak on issues of national importance. The question of investment in South Africa is one such issue. We call for a National Convention in which the Blacks in South Africa can speak for themselves on the matter of foreign investment.

Today, the 10th of March 1976,
the above statement is published in South Africa.

A National Convention on Christian Concern for Southern Africa

A RESPONSE BY WHITE CHURCHMEN

REQUEST FOR BLACK LEADERSHIP

1. With deep interest and joy we welcome the speech of Chief Gatsha Buthelezi at Jubalani Amphitheatre, Soweto, on March 14, 1976. It is a courageous and reconciliatory call to a revolution in attitudes which warrants a positive response.

2. We realise that the kind of response required in these circumstances is not easy for the majority of white Christians, whether clerical or lay. They have not been prepared for it by a church which, through historical circumstances, has too long neglected the social and political implications of the Gospel. It is only in the last generation or two that the Christian conscience, at a significantly widespread level, has begun to stir in this direction.

3. The Chief's astute call is the true recognition by a Christian layman that God summons Christians to a new involvement and commitment in these days of portent. God is calling his people to Christian liberation, that is, to an acceptance of the law of love, not only between individuals in limited communities, but also between communities themselves, between races, nations and classes. Black liberation, and the consequent liberation of whites, which blacks fervently desire, are fundamental activities of this law of love.

4. We do not believe that the Church can be defended by retreating into traditional practices, or by concentrating on its own internal affairs, or in the futile endeavour to persuade the establishment to apply apartheid kindly. Such attitudes have largely destroyed the credibility of the Church. The Gospel of Christ is vital in our age. The Church of Christ will regain its vitality as it commits its manpower and resources to obey the gospel initiatives to bring life in all its aspects, personal and political, into harmony with the standards of His Kingdom.

5. All Christians are called to devote themselves to set all men free in all ways through the truth of Christ in this subcontinent. In this critical hour we recognise that Christians are called to act in decisive repentance, and to move into the stormy areas of political, economic, and social life with the gospel imperatives of justice and reconciliation for all people. They are summoned to give themselves to a fundamental change in our public life, exposing evil, and following Christ through the turmoil of events where he makes himself known. A new understanding of Christian social life is at hand.

6. The leaders of Southern Africa desperately require the true insights of the Christian gospel in daily affairs as they seek the narrow road to life. These insights could well be expressed in a National Convention on Christian concern for Southern Africa. We are confident that the Black Christians of our land, with true prophetic vision, will take the initiative to which they have been urged, that all of us might follow.

> Timothy Bavin
> Denis E. Hurley
> C. F. Beyers Naudé

> (Supplement to *Pro Veritate*, March 1976)

Easter Message, 1977

In South Africa Christian witness for truth, justice and liberation is under strong pressure.

Governmental legislation for race and colour is completely opposite to Christ's commandment about man and society.

The protest of many Christians against the injustice and violence is answered with unrestricted detention, "bannings" and loss of the means to an income.

Race policy threatens Christian brotherhood, church unity, as well as the carrying out of Christ's commandment regarding mission and Christian service.

More and more the power of the state is coming into conflict with the powerlessness of the church.

The self-assurance of the power of the state is reflected in what Pilate said to Jesus: "Why don't you speak to me? Don't you know I have the power to crucify you and the power to let you free?"

Jesus' death apparently confirms the complete power of the authorities: the state has the final word. But Jesus answers: "You would not have any power over me unless it had been given to you from above." And his resurrection confirms his word "to me has been given all power . . ."

Therefore our hearts rejoice and we celebrate Easter in S.A., because we know: The heavy oppression and the approaching storm is the necessary way of suffering which precedes the joy of a new Easter where we as Christians of all races will experience the glorious truth: "to me is given all power in heaven and on earth."

Dr. C.F. Beyers Naudé
April 4th, 1977

Naudé's last published speech before his banning
To the Transvaal United
Teachers' Association.

We are living in the midst of the most crucial period of South African history; we are either contributing to the further enslavement of our total society or its eventual liberation. As teachers we could either use and positively exploit our strategic position or, in refusing to do so, remain part of the problem instead of becoming part of the movement of true human liberation. My urgent appeal to you as a teaching profession is this: Let your voices be heard, let your actions be seen as part of the contribution which you are making towards the liberation of the Christian faith, the Christian church and the total society.

During the last few years, however, a subtle but very definite shift in evaluation of the authority of the church, the Christian faith and the teaching profession has taken place in Black society. This important change can be attributed to a number of reasons, the most important being the political situation in our country and the sudden awakening of urban youth. The support for the government policy of apartheid which a powerful church like the white Dutch Reformed Church (but also other churches) gave, inevitably led the Black people to conclude that the Christian faith, being the white man's faith, was identical to racial oppression. Christianity was seen by millions of Blacks to be equated with racial discrimination, oppressive legislation, denial of human dignity, denial of political rights and relegation into a permanently subservient position because of one's skin. Because the policy of apartheid enjoyed divine sanction as far as the whites were concerned, a strong movement of rejection of the church and even of the Christian faith has taken place amongst many, many young Blacks. . . . In a short period the tables were turned: traditional Christianity as presented and propagated by whites and Blacks was put on trial. A crisis of credibility of the Christian faith has arrived.